Islamism and Fundamentalism in the Modern World

Lilah el-Sayed

MASON CREST
PHILADELPHIA

Mason Crest
450 Parkway Drive, Suite D
Broomall, PA 19008
www.masoncrest.com

©2017 by Mason Crest, an imprint of National Highlights, Inc.

Printed and bound in the United States of America.

CPSIA Compliance Information: Batch #UI2016.
For further information, contact Mason Crest at 1-866-MCP-Book.

First printing
1 3 5 7 9 8 6 4 2

Library of Congress Cataloging-in-Publication Data

on file at the Library of Congress
ISBN: 978-1-4222-3673-4 (hc)
ISBN: 978-1-4222-8111-6 (ebook)

Understanding Islam series ISBN: 978-1-4222-3670-3

Table of Contents

KEY ICONS TO LOOK FOR:

Text-Dependent Questions: These questions send the reader back to the text for more careful attention to the evidence presented there.

Words to Understand: These words with their easy-to-understand definitions will increase the reader's understanding of the text, while building vocabulary skills.

Series Glossary of Key Terms: This back-of-the book glossary contains terminology used throughout this series. Words found here increase the reader's ability to read and comprehend higher-level books and articles in this field.

Research Projects: Readers are pointed toward areas of further inquiry connected to each chapter. Suggestions are provided for projects that encourage deeper research and analysis.

Sidebars: This boxed material within the main text allows readers to build knowledge, gain insights, explore possibilities, and broaden their perspectives by weaving together additional information to provide realistic and holistic perspectives.

Introduction

by Camille Pecastaing, Ph.D.

Islam needs no introduction. Everyone around the world old enough is likely to have a formed opinion of Islam and Muslims. The cause of this wide recognition is, sadly, the recurrent eruptions of violence that have marred the recent—and not so recent—history of the Muslim world. A violence that has also selectively followed Muslim immigrants to foreign lands, and placed Islam at the front and center of global issues.

Notoriety is why Islam needs no simple introduction, but far more than that. Islam needs a correction, an exposition, a full discussion of its origins, its principles, its history, and of course of what it means to the 1.5 to 2 billion contemporaries associated with it, whether by origins, tradition, practice or belief.

The challenge is that Islam has a long history, spread over fourteen centuries. Its principles have been contested from the beginning, the religion has known schism after schism, and politico-theological issues instructed all sorts of violent conflict. The history of Islam is epic, leaving Islam today as a mosaic of diverse sects and practices: Sunnism, Shi'ism, Sufism, Salafism, Wahhabism, and of course, Jihadism. The familiarity of those terms often masks ignorance of the distinctions between them.

Islam is many things to many people, and while violent radicals occupy the headlines, what a Muslim is in the 21st century is practically indefinable. Islam is present on every continent; the religion of billionaires and of the poorest people in the world, the religion of kings and revolutionaries, of illiterate pastoralists and nuclear scientists, of fundamentalist theologians and avant-garde artists. Arabic is the language of Islam, the language of the Qur'an, but most Muslims only speak other tongues. Many Muslims indulge in moderate consumption of alcohol without feeling that they have renounced their faith. Boiled down to its simplest expression, being Muslim in the 21st century is an appreciation for one's origins and a reluctance to eat pork.

It is not only non-Muslims who have a partial view of Islam. Muslims, too, have a point of view limited by their own experience. This tunnel vision is often blamed for the radicalization that takes place at the margins of Islam. It is because they do not fully apprehend the diversity and complexity of their faith that some follow the extremist views of preachers of doom and violence. Among those, many are converts, or secularized Muslims who knew and cared little about religion until they embraced radicalism. Conversely, the foundation of deradicalization programs is education: teaching former militants about the complexity of the Islamic tradition, in particular the respect for the law and tolerance of diversity that Prophet Muhammad showed when he was the ruler of Medinah.

Islam in the 21st century is a political religion. There are four Islamic republics, and other states that have made Islam their official religion, bringing Islamic law (Shari'a) in varying degrees into their legal systems. Wherever multiparty elections are held, from Morocco to Indonesia, there are parties representing political Islam. Some blame Islam's political claims for the relative decline of the Muslim world. Once a center of wealth and power and knowledge, it now lags behind its European and East Asian neighbors, still struggling to transition from a rural, agrarian way of life to the urban, now post-industrial age. But for others, only Islam will deliver a successful and indigenous modernization.

Islam is also an economic actor. Shari'a instructs the practices of what is known as Islamic finance, a sector of the international financial system that oversees two trillion dollars worth of assets. For decades now, Islamist organizations have palliated the deficiencies of regional states in the provision of social services, from education to healthcare, counseling, emergency relief, and assistance to find employment. It is the reach of Islamist grassroots networks that has insured the recent electoral success of Islamic parties. Where the Arab Spring brought liberalization and democratization, Islam was given more space in society, not less.

It should be clear to all by now that modernity, and postmodernity, is not absolute convergence toward a single model—call it the Western, secular, democratic model. Islam is not a legacy from a backward past that refuses to die, it is also a claim to shape the future in a new way. Post-communist China is making a similar claim, and there may be others to come, although today none is as forcefully and sometimes as brutally articulated as Islam's. That only would justify the urgency to learn about Islam, deconstruct simplistic stereotypes and educate oneself to the diversity of the world.

1

Defining Islamic Fundamentalism

Islam is the youngest of the major world religions, but it is also the fastest growing: in many areas of the world, including Europe and the United States, the number of Muslims is increasing rapidly. In this global context, Muslims exhibit as many differences among themselves as do Christians. Different groups of Muslims express and practice their beliefs in different ways.

Muslims do, however, hold some common beliefs and consider themselves a worldwide community (*umma*) unified in devotion to Allah. (Allah is the Arabic word for God.) Regardless of where they live, Muslims share a faith in a single God and revere their holy text, the Qur'an. They also take very seriously both their moral responsibility and their accountability before God, and they believe their faith should inform all areas of life.

The belief that religion cannot be separated from any other part of life was an important part of the teachings of the prophet

Opposite: Broadly speaking, Islamic fundamentalists advocate a return to their religion's seventh-century roots, and they want Islam to be the organizing principle for all aspects of life, including politics, law, and social relations. Beyond these and a few other shared goals, however, the character of Islamic fundamentalism tends to vary by region and culture.

Muhammad in the seventh century, and for hundreds of years this belief buttressed a great Islamic civilization that extended its power through the Middle East and into Asia, Africa, and Europe. But the rise of European power and the era of Western *colonialism* in the 18th, 19th, and 20th centuries eroded Islamic institutions and the long tradition of cultural and intellectual unity among Muslims, leading to a sense of powerlessness and loss. In this new context, Muslims adapted differing viewpoints on the role of Islam in political and social life.

During the colonial period, Muslims developed a range of responses to Western expansion. Muslim reformers argued that Muslims should not simply accept or reject Western ideals, but should reinterpret traditional Islamic institutions and law in order to adapt to the contemporary situation. These Muslims were known broadly as Islamic modernists. Other thinkers and activists argued that the only path to survival and prosperity in the modern era was to fully Westernize, to adopt *secular* modes of government and public life. Others began to call for a return to the roots of the Islamic faith as a way to recover a sense of identity and reclaim power for Muslim societies. They said that the only way to revitalize Muslim societies was to reestablish religious legal authority in every sphere of life. These Muslims have been widely referred to as Islamic fundamentalists, and their response to the pressures of modernity gained momentum during the 20th century.

In response to the decline of Islamic political and cultural power, fundamentalists blame Muslims themselves for straying from the straight path of Islam. They also say secular political and

 Words to Understand in This Chapter

colonialism—a system in which one country creates an empire by taking over other lands and creating colonies that provide resources and money to the mother country.
secular—attitudes, activities, or other things that have no religious or spiritual basis.

Islamic fundamentalism arose in part as a reaction against Western political and cultural dominance. Today ambivalence toward Western—and, in particular, U.S.—influences pervades many Arab societies.

moral systems (particularly from the West) are unjust and bankrupt and that they erode Islamic institutions and the Muslim way of life. Islamic fundamentalists want to rid their religion of all such corruption, both among Muslims themselves and from external influences. In theory, they see any innovation in Islam beyond the practices set forth by Muhammad and his earliest followers in the seventh century, as well as all non-Muslim practices, as a potential threat to their faith. Fundamentalists propose Islam as a comprehensive system that governs all of life, and many of them support the idea of national government based on the *Sharia* (Islamic law). Since the mid-1900s, and particularly since the 1960s, these fundamentalist views have had enormous effects on Muslims themselves and on political and social realities in countries around the world.

But while fundamentalists decry reformist and modernist Muslims' openness to the West, their own approaches have sometimes themselves been shaped by Western ideals. This is perhaps nowhere more evident than in contemporary attitudes toward the

Sharia. Through the centuries, most Muslims have viewed the Sharia not as a code of fixed rules that govern behavior, but rather as the path toward knowledge of God's will and the way to achieve God's justice on earth. The Sharia includes not only rules, but also the methods of interpretation judges use to determine those rules; throughout the Islamic world, judges deal with important issues in local Muslim communities and develop interpretations based on the Qur'an and the example of the prophet Muhammad relevant to the context. The Sharia is not a codified, fixed set of laws enforced by a central government. However, with the advent of the nation-state and colonialism—together with the idea of a standard, fixed law written for an entire country—some Muslims' ideas about the Sharia also changed. Many fundamentalists came to view the Sharia as a fixed set of laws that should uniformly govern an entire nation. The Sharia as a fixed entity then increasingly took on a symbolic role as fundamentalists sought to build support against Western cultural and political control in Muslim countries.

Because Muslims believe the Qur'an records the exact words of God, great emphasis is placed on studying, memorizing, and reciting the holy book in the classical Arabic in which it was originally revealed to the prophet Muhammad. That language can be difficult to master, even for native speakers of modern Arabic. Shown here is a Qur'an student in Djenné, a town in the West African country of Mali.

The Fundamentalist Worldview

While defining Islamic fundamentalism as a whole is a useful exercise, it is helpful to remember that the phenomenon takes as many different shapes within Islam as do culturally specific Islamic expressions of faith. Fundamentalists do not all share the same socioeconomic background, nor do they subscribe to one global set of objectives. Modern fundamentalism is not a movement exclusively, or even predominantly, of the poor, uneducated, and marginalized within the Islamic world. Rather, it flourishes particularly among the educated middle classes and in certain respects is a product of the spread of literacy. Nor do all fundamentalists strive for the same political goals. Many join moderate political parties to seek changes through the government; a relative few, such as the extremist Osama bin Laden, vow to wage war at all costs against both non-Muslims and any Muslims thought to support Western ideals and governments.

It is also important to understand the complex historical context in which contemporary Islamic fundamentalism developed. After the end of European colonialism in the Islamic world, the growth of fundamentalism was hastened by numerous events: the founding of the State of Israel in 1948, U.S. intervention in the Middle East, the end of the Cold War, the failure of nationalist governments in the Arab world, and the process of globalization, in which clear distinctions between the East and the West have disappeared.

In contrast to fundamentalists, modernists seek an environment in which modern ideas can coexist with Muslim ideals and faith. Many moderate modernists appeal directly to the Qur'an, the *Hadith* (the body of traditions and sayings ascribed to Muhammad), and Islamic history to advocate democracy, human rights, and a largely secular society. Secularists, in contrast, seek to distance government from Islamic institutions and to embrace completely nonreligious models of national identity and economic development.

But fundamentalism and modernism are both responses to pressures on Islam in the modern world—pressures from without to accept secular views of the relationship between society, government, and religion, and pressures from within to refuse to change centuries-old traditions in the face of contemporary realities. Modernists seek to accommodate new ideas within Islam, while fundamentalists seek to return to the core vision of Islam they believe to be set forth in the Qur'an and Hadith.

Defining the Key Terms

The term *fundamentalism* actually refers to any effort to purify a religion by laying out the fundamentals of that religion and expecting individuals and even whole societies to abide by them. Fundamentalists have emerged in every major religion in the modern era. The term *fundamentalism* was in fact coined to describe the call for a return to the roots of Christianity made by some Protestant Christians in the United States during the 1920s. It came into wide use for Islamic groups only after the Iranian revolution in 1979.

Though *fundamentalism* is still a widely used term for the modern efforts to purify Islam, other terms are used frequently as well. These include *revivalism, Islamism, resurgence, traditionalism,* and *renewal*. Increasingly, *Islamism* is used in journalistic and scholarly accounts of the phenomenon. *Fundamentalism* is often used interchangeably with *militant extremism,* but the latter term refers specifically to the beliefs of fundamentalist groups who advocate violence as a means to bring about their proposed reforms. These militant groups are a minority among Islamic fundamentalists. Most fundamentalists work through religious institutions and political parties to enact changes peacefully.

Another term widely associated with Islamic fundamentalism is the Arabic word *jihad*, which is often interpreted to mean "holy war" but literally translates as "struggle" and has a long and complex history of use within Islam. In fact, the legal scholars (*ulama*) who formulated most of Islamic law by the 11th century did not specify the concept of jihad as holy war. The Qur'an simply calls Muslims to "struggle in the path of God." Traditionally, the ulama distinguished between the Greater Jihad, which is the effort of the individual to become a better Muslim, and the Lesser Jihad, which referred to the struggle against enemies to defend the oppressed and establish justice. The majority of the *ulama* argued that Muslims should fight others only when they threaten Muslims. The *ulama* did, however, condemn any who acted with indiscriminate violence. The *ulama* called these rebels *muharibs* ("those who fight society") and defined them as terrorists who secretly carry out violent acts against innocent people and thus keep the entire society in fear.

However, as colonialism eroded traditional institutions and beliefs and as secular, nationalist governments further undermined the role of Islamic authority, the conditions emerged for a new, more militant definition of *jihad*. Increasing incursions by Western powers led to a loss of self-esteem among Muslims at large. The resulting despair spurred many young Muslims to seek justice. Thus, the new definition of *jihad* as "holy war" pointedly illustrates the political nature of contemporary Islamic fundamentalism as it has taken shape in the past 40 years.

 # Text-Dependent Questions

1. What is Sharia?
2. What is the difference between modernists and fundamentalists?

 # Research Project

Muslims believe that the Qur'an is the divine messages of Allah to all humankind, which He revealed to the Prophet Muhammad in the early seventh century. The Qur'an was passed down orally or preserved as separate sayings during Muhammad's lifetime, and an authoritative written version was not compiled until many years after the Prophet's death. Using the Internet or your school library, find out more about the Qur'an. How is this scripture structured? How was it preserved by the original Muslim communities? Write a two-page report and share your findings with the class.

2

Islamic Fundamentalism in the Modern Age

From the time of Muhammad, Muslims believed that the faithfulness of the *umma* resulted in the expansion of Islamic civilization. But after the enormous territorial and cultural gains of the Abbasid period (750–1258), the empire broke into a scattered collection of kingdoms. Battles with the Europeans during the Crusades in the 11th and 12th centuries and with the Mongols in the 13th century left Islamic forces in further disarray.

Around 1300, however, a new Islamic power began to rise: the Ottoman Empire. From their home base in Anatolia in what is now Turkey, the Ottomans spread their influence outward in a series of conquests. By the mid-1500s the Ottoman Empire stretched from the Middle East and North Africa through Mesopotamia and southeastern Europe. Although a significant number of Muslims remained outside Ottoman rule—especially in India, Iran (Persia), and parts of Africa and Southeast Asia—the empire was the center of Islamic civilization and power for hundreds of years. Within it were the holy

Opposite: Egyptians gather in Tahrir Square, Cairo, in January 2012 to celebrate the success of Islamist candidates in the country's first democratic election after the overthrow of longtime ruler Hosni Mubarak. The Muslim Brotherhood, the country's leading Islamist party, won more than half the seats in the parliamentary election.

cities of Mecca, Medina, and Jerusalem and the leading cultural centers of Istanbul, Baghdad, Cairo, and Damascus.

By 1600, European nations had begun to seriously challenge the power of the Ottoman Empire. Over the next three centuries, the Europeans would wear down and ultimately eclipse the Ottomans militarily and commercially.

Changes in the global economy, as well as European innovations, helped tip the balance in favor of Europe. With advances in navigation and shipping, the traditional silk routes through the Middle East and Central Asia, which the Ottomans controlled, were no longer vital. Exploration and colonization of the Americas resulted in an influx of cheap resources, and industrialization shifted commercial power to Europe. The *sultans* of the Ottoman Empire found themselves increasingly in debt to European powers, and on the battlefield their military forces had little success against the more sophisticated weaponry developed by the Europeans.

By the late 1700s, Western ideas began to seep into the empire as Europeans continued to expand their military and commercial power at the expense of the Ottomans. Many among the *ulama* concluded that Muslims had strayed from the straight path of Islam. To turn back the Europeans, they believed, Muslims would have to return to their faith.

From their origins in the seventh century, the *ulama* had developed into a special Muslim class, with the authority to study the

 Words to Understand in This Chapter

ayatollah—a religious leader of Shiite Muslims.

caliphate—the dominion of the chief Muslim ruler, who is regarded as a successor of Muhammad.

fatwa—a legal opinion or decree issued by an Islamic religious leader.

sultan—a ruler of a Muslim country.

Qur'an and the Hadith and discern God's will for the Islamic community. The *ulama* are not priests, but laymen trained in religious doctrine and prepared to transmit it. As Islam developed and spread, the *ulama* relied on the Sharia as they made legal rulings governing all aspects of Muslim life, which they applied as judges. The *ulama* became the leaders of Islam's mosques and seminaries and had extensive control in a vast religion that functioned with little central organization. As Western thought and customs continued to filter into the Ottoman Empire through the 1800s, however, the *ulama* found themselves increasingly isolated and their powers reduced until they were confined to issuing legal opinions on personal life only.

Meanwhile, as European powers occupied Muslim territories—the French in North Africa, the Russians in Central Asia, the British in Egypt and India, the Dutch in Southeast Asia—the Ottoman Empire implemented military and bureaucratic reforms and went through a series of failed experiments with Western-style representative government. By 1900 much of the Muslim world was under some form of European control, and World War I finally swept away the remnants of the Ottoman Empire two decades later. With Britain and France splitting the remaining Ottoman lands after the war, the last Islamic empire had been destroyed. The global Muslim community was devastated by the loss.

During the Ottoman Empire's long decline, Islamic thinkers and activists had tried to envision a path back to Islam's former glory. By the late 19th century, both modernist and fundamentalist responses to the crisis in Islam were emerging. They shared the ultimate goal of beating back Western expansion but differed greatly in approach. The modernists sought to forge a relationship between Islam and Western models of government and development. Islamic legal reformers joined this trend, which in the end actually eroded the influence of the Sharia, Islamic judges, and the *ulama*. The fundamentalists, by contrast, organized in opposition to it.

The Reformers

The roots of Islamic modernism are epitomized in the work of certain key thinkers, all of whom insisted that Muslims needed to reform their traditions in order to regain their lost power. These thinkers believed Islam could use Western patterns of government because similar patterns had in fact once been central to Islamic rule, but had been lost through the years.

Jamal al-Din Afghani (1838–1897), a Persian, traveled widely among Islamic lands and often supported groups resistant to European expansion and control. He said that scientific inquiry had been a key part of Islamic civilization and that eliminating it was in part to blame for the decline in Islam's status. Rather than reject Western scientific advances, Afghani wanted Muslims and the *ulama* in particular to locate the secrets of Western strength and use them to their advantage. He also advocated for parliamentary forms of government, which he identified with the traditional Islamic practice of consultation (*shura*), as well as a new emphasis on science and technology.

Afghani maintained that Muslims must remain rooted in the practices set forth by Muhammad and the first believers (*salafiyya*). He did not suggest, however, a simple return to the traditional interpretations of Islam, but rather advocated new interpretations that would enable Muslims to respond to their changing world. He sought to reintroduce the concept of *ijtihad*, individual interpretation of the law, and to replace the practice of *taqlid*, the simple imitation of the law as set forth by the *ulama* in the first several centuries after Muhammad. The practice of *ijtihad* would enable Muslims to preserve their core traditions while reinterpreting sections of the law to reflect modern realities.

With support from the Ottoman sultan, Afghani proposed a Pan-Islamic coalition of countries and regions that reflected the idea of the *umma*. He saw this as important because in their colonies the Europeans were establishing the boundaries of future nation-states, a foreign concept in lands once united under the rule of Islamic empires. He believed Muslims must reassert their unity in order to adapt to the pressures of the modern era.

Afghani's Egyptian student Muhammad Abduh (1849–1905) was a leading member of the *ulama* who said that faith and reason go hand in hand and that the decline of Islam could be blamed on the unwillingness of the *ulama* to consider new interpretations of tradition. Abduh maintained that certain laws (especially those regarding worship) should go unchanged but that laws about family and society should be reinterpreted with changing historical conditions. He proposed more education for women, for example, and argued against polygamy.

Like Afghani and his followers, India's Sayyid Ahmad Khan (1817–1898) proposed a reinterpretation of Islamic traditions, but he went one step further: rather than suggesting that Islam could coexist with reason and science, he believed Islam, reason, and science were inextricably bound together and thus the Qur'an and Hadith should be interpreted in light of modern scientific thinking. His political analysis, however, did not stretch beyond British rule in India. He thought any attempts at Pan-Islamic unity were not feasible, and he suggested that Indian Muslims needed to accept and adapt to the reality of British power in their country, something for which Afghani criticized him.

These modernist reformers all proposed a reinterpretation of Islam rather than an uncritical acceptance of tradition, and they sought a synthesis of Islamic tenets and the scientific and intellectual developments of modernity. From North Africa east to Indonesia, modernists acted on their ideas with mixed results. Melding tradition with modern ideas was not easy in practice, especially since the conservative *ulama* still governed the academic and legal institutions of Islam, which gave the reformers no platform for enacting their ideas. It was also difficult to develop leadership roles among the secularists, who ended up heading the new Muslim countries. In most nation-states gaining their independence from colonial powers, secular legislatures set up the legal codes.

The Roots of the Fundamentalist Response

The argument that Muslims must not stray from the straight path of Islam is almost as old as Islam itself. Only 25 years after the prophet Muhammad's death, the Kharijis became the first dissenters in Islam, asserting a literal interpretation of the Qur'an and an ultra-strict delineation between Muslims, who prove their faith in their behavior, and non-Muslims. In the Kharijis' view, Muslims who were seen to have compromised their faith had to be excluded from the Islamic community and could even be punished by death.

As Islamic institutions and law developed over the following centuries, many religious reformers (*mujaddids*) appealed to this vision of "pure" Islam. Dismayed by the Mongols' defeat of the Abbasid **Caliphate**, the legal scholar Taqi al-Din Ahmad ibn Taymiyya (1268–1328) called for a strict, literal interpretation of the Qur'an and Hadith as the only way to restore Islamic purity and Islamic power. He issued a legal opinion (**fatwa**) condemning the Mongols because they professed Islam but did not follow the Sharia and calling on faithful Muslims not to obey their Mongol rulers.

Ibn Taymiyya's fatwa greatly affected the thinking of Muhammad ibn Abd al-Wahhab (1703–1792). Al-Wahhab was highly critical of what he saw as corruption in Islamic society on the Arabian Peninsula, which he said had returned to a pre-Islamic state of ignorance. He called for a literal interpretation of the Qur'an, considered most of the Sharia a corruption of authentic Islam, and did not recognize the legitimacy of the long-established schools of Islamic law. Al-Wahhab called for *ijtihad*, and indeed his emphasis on this concept foreshadowed the work of Muslim reformers like Afghani and Abduh. Al-Wahhab's goal, however, was not to reform Islam to reflect new ideas and practices, but rather to return the Islamic way of life to the "golden age" of Islam, when Muhammad and his companions in Medina set forth infallible codes of belief and conduct. Al-Wahhab and the Arabian tribal chief Muhammad ibn Saud declared war on all people they considered unfaithful to true Islam. Though defeated by the Ottoman Empire, they laid the foundation for the modern state of Saudi Arabia and set an example that would inspire later fundamentalist groups.

Throughout the 19th century, numerous rebellions against colonial powers used Islamic language and symbols to legitimize their cause, while other movements actively called for a return to pure Islam as part of their struggle. In West Africa, for instance, fundamentalist movements organized with the goal of returning Islam to political power and enforcing strict adherence to the Sharia. In countries like Nigeria, Somalia, and Sudan, fundamentalists staged reform efforts and outright rebellions, most of which were brutally suppressed. Similar rebellions occurred in India and western China.

Into the 20th Century

The Western colonial presence continued in much of the Muslim world into the early 1900s. Twentieth-century fundamentalism first developed in response to Western colonialism and strengthened as Muslim modernists developed patterns of self-rule using nationalist, secular models.

The Muslim Brotherhood took the lead in the Arab world. It was established in Egypt in 1928 by Hasan al-Banna (1906–1949), who used Islamic symbols to build greater unity among Egyptians in resistance to the British colonial presence and later developed extensive social programs for Egyptians living under independent but secular rule. The Islamic Society of India, founded in 1941 by Mawlana Mawdudi (1903–1979), shared much the same approach.

After independence, many of the new countries used Western parliamentary forms of government; some aligned themselves with democratic capitalism (such as Turkey and Tunisia), while others developed forms of socialism (such as Egypt, Syria, Iraq, and Libya).

The new nationalist governments understood the influence of Islam in society—many leaders appealed to citizens by using Islamic language and symbols—but they kept the walls between politics and religion intact. In only a few countries did Islamic religious authorities legitimize monarchies (Morocco, Jordan, Oman, and the Malayan States) or retain real power (Yemen, Saudi Arabia).

In the aftermath of colonial domination, however, the new secular governments struggled, beset by corruption, mismanagement, and continued Western influence. High unemployment and poverty rates increased the feelings of loss and low self-esteem among Muslim citizens, while the rapid pace of modernization jeopardized traditional Islamic values and practices.

Both al-Banna and Mawdudi opposed the *ulama* for collaborating with secular governments, and the modernist reformers for relying too much on Western ideals. Both argued that every realm of life should be directed by Islamic principles. Al-Banna established the Muslim Brotherhood when he was only 22, arguing that the *ulama* had failed to resist the spiritual decay and foreign values brought by Westernization. Furthermore, he maintained, while Britain had granted Egypt's independence in 1922, it still controlled the country.

Al-Banna assailed the new Egyptian government's corruption, and, though he was not against democracy itself, he thought the Western patterns of government the Egyptian leaders had imported were imposing values that common Egyptians did not share. Islam and the Qur'an offered everything Muslims needed, said al-Banna, so they did not need to turn to the West for ideas about how to govern their society. He also condemned the materialism he saw in both capitalist and communist societies, asserting that it threatened Muslims' spiritual well-being even as it created deep divisions between the ruling elite and average citizens. He emphasized nonviolent jihad as the only way to bring revival to Muslims and return Islam to its rightful place in the world. In its appeal to Egyptian Muslims as a whole, the Muslim Brotherhood under al-Banna founded broad social welfare programs to provide an Islamic alternative to the Egyptian government.

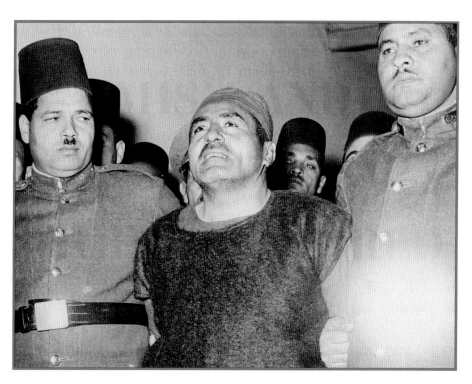

A member of Egypt's Muslim Brotherhood is led to the gallows following his conviction for a 1954 plot to assassinate President Gamal Abdel Nasser. Nasser banned the fundamentalist organization and ordered a ruthless crackdown on its members, but the Brotherhood remained a significant force in Egyptian society.

Mawdudi was driven in large part by his concern that Indian Muslims be granted independence to govern their own affairs and not be subsumed in a new Hindu-dominated, secular Indian government. He maintained that Islam and nationalism were incompatible, and that their faith alone bound Muslims together as a community. In the beginning, he did not support the creation of Pakistan as a solution to the Indian Muslim problem, for he rightly realized that it, too, would be a secular experiment. Unlike al-Banna, Mawdudi always envisioned change from the top down, arguing until his death for an Islamic state in Pakistan. Perhaps Mawdudi's central contribution to later fundamentalist movements was his interpretation of the concept of jihad as the struggle for a Muslim revolution in the entire world order.

The governments of Egypt and Pakistan saw the Muslim Brotherhood and the Islamic Society, respectively, as a radical threat to their secular rule. The Egyptian secret police killed al-Banna in 1949. Egyptian president Gamal Abdel Nasser outlawed the Muslim Brotherhood in 1954. Nasser ordered the imprisonment and torture of numerous Brotherhood leaders and members. Later, after a period of revival under Anwar Sadat, the group was partially banned again. In Pakistan, Mawdudi was kept under surveillance and spent time in prison on several occasions.

Both al-Banna and Mawdudi influenced Sayyid Qutb (1906–1966), a prominent member of the Egyptian Muslim Brotherhood. In his books *In the Shade of the Qur'an*, a multi-volume commentary on the Qur'an, and *Milestones*, Qutb provided an in-depth response to the tensions between Islam and the West. Qutb extended Mawdudi's assessment that Western societies were ignorant (*jahili*) of God's will because of their lack of Islamic rule, and as the Egyptian government brutally suppressed the Muslim Brotherhood, he eventually concluded that leaders of Muslim countries also encouraged *jahiliyyah* and must be forcibly removed from power. Qutb based his thinking in part on time he spent in the United States, where he was appalled by what he saw as unbridled materialism, sexual promiscuity, and racism. Qutb also felt that U.S. support for the new state of Israel came at the expense of Muslim interests.

Qutb did not hesitate to identify those committed to Islamic rule as good and those opposed as evil, and the Egyptian government was so concerned about the spread of his radical vision that it declared any citizen caught with a copy of *Milestones* liable for treason. After 10 years in prison, Qutb was executed in 1966 under order from Nasser. His intelligent writings and his refusal to give in to Nasser (he could have avoided death by recanting his writings) remain a strong influence on radical fundamentalists today. His influence is also felt among Muslims in general; *In the Shade of the Qur'an* is still widely read throughout the Islamic world by Muslims of diverse backgrounds and beliefs.

Fundamentalism After 1960

By the 1960s, frustration with the failures of secular rule in the Muslim world—government corruption, false promises of democracy, ongoing unemployment and poverty—as well as Israel's growing power had eroded Muslim confidence so much that the fundamentalist appeal took on new momentum.

In June 1967, Israel defeated the combined forces of Egypt, Jordan, and Syria in the Six-Day War, creating new longings among Arabs for the glories of past Islamic civilizations. Egypt's modest successes in the 1973 October War with Israel, together with Arab states' imposition of an oil embargo that same year, kindled hope for a new era of Islamic power. But more than any other event, the Iranian revolution of 1979 inspired those Muslims who sought Islamic renewal. When young militants forced the pro-West shah of Iran into exile and swept the *Ayatollah* Ruhollah Khomeini into power, giving rise to a new Islamic state, great numbers of Muslims rededicated themselves to daily prayer and the Muslim holy days.

Muslims longing for Islamic renewal also developed Islamic media outlets and established reformist Islamic groups, including political parties. Community-based organizations like the Muslim Brotherhood and university student groups increased in size and influence, widening their grassroots work and calling for a gradual conversion to Islamic values and government. Many conservative *ulama*—for instance, those of Cairo's al-Azhar Mosque University —began to advocate the return to pure forms of Islam. At least on a superficial level, secular governments also responded; leaders in numerous Muslim countries increasingly appealed to Islam to enhance their legitimacy and popular support.

Non-militant fundamentalist Islamic organizations increased their participation in the political process in the 1980s and 1990s. They participated in elections, and in some cases their candidates were elected to high national office. They focused on international issues as well, their top concern being Israel's occupation of Palestinian territories. They also protested the Soviet Union's occupation of Afghanistan, United Nations sanctions against Iraq after the Gulf War, and government repression of Muslims in Bosnia, Chechnya, and Kashmir.

In the meantime, however, militant groups also flourished, attracting new recruits across the Muslim world and especially in Egypt, Lebanon, and Palestine. In Egypt numerous secret groups plotted to overthrow their own government. Muhammad al-Faraj, a member of the group Islamic Jihad, relied heavily on Ibn Taymiyya and Qutb in his manifesto *The Neglected Duty*, in which he interpreted jihad as a violent struggle against corrupt society. He spoke of jihad as the forgotten sixth pillar of Islam and called for armed revolution to overthrow Egypt's secular leaders and install an Islamic state.

Iran backed some militant groups, including Hizbollah, which fought the Israeli occupation of Lebanese territories in the 1980s. The groups Hamas and Islamic Jihad formed in the Israeli-occupied West Bank and Gaza Strip to fight for a Palestinian state and began

In 1979 massive street protests in Tehran and other Iranian cities helped topple the secular, pro-U.S. regime of Mohammad Reza Pahlavi and bring to power a government dominated by conservative Shiite clerics.

dispatching suicide bombers to attack Israeli targets. And in Afghanistan, the Wahhabist mindset of Osama bin Laden and other U.S.-backed rebels ignited a new militancy in the Arabs who had gathered there to fight Soviet occupation. Bin Laden later became the leader of al-Qaeda, which carried out the September 11, 2001, suicide attacks on the United States. These groups made up only a small minority of Muslim fundamentalists, but the threat they posed to their own and Western countries in the eyes of many overshadowed the quiet work done by less radical fundamentalist groups.

A closer examination of the full range of the work of fundamentalist groups, both moderate and militant, in different Muslim countries and regions will provide a more complete understanding of just how modern fundamentalism has affected Muslims and how Western governments have responded to it.

 Text-Dependent Questions

1. Who was Muhammad ibn Abd al-Wahhab? What was his goal?
2. What Egyptian organization did Hasan al-Banna establish in 1928?

 Research Project

Using the Internet or your school library, find out more about the Muslim Brotherhood, the largest Islamist organization in Egypt. Write a two-page report about this organization and it's impact on Egyptian life and society, and present it to your class.

3

The Iranian Revolution

As followers of Shia Islam, Iranians had long seen themselves as a separate people with a tradition of fighting injustice, and they set themselves further apart by taking on the West and developing a popular movement for an Islamic state. The Iranian revolution of 1979 in turn did more than any other event in modern-day Islam to spread fundamentalism through the global Islamic community and alert the rest of the world to its influence.

History of Iran

With the advent of the Safavid dynasty in 1501, Iran (long called Persia) became a unified independent state. The first leader of the dynasty declared himself *shah* (king), a title dating from the pre-Islamic era, and proclaimed Twelver Shiism the official religion. Patriotism came easily to the Iranians because they were sharply aware of their pre-Islamic history and maintained their own language

Opposite: Large crowds turned out for this rally in Tehran marking the 22nd anniversary of Iran's Islamic Revolution. But by the early years of the 21st century, dissatisfaction with the government's restrictive social policies and economic mismanagement was believed to be widespread, particularly among the young.

(Persian). For the next 150 years, Iran fought the Sunni-dominated Ottoman Empire for control over the Middle East.

The shahs developed very extravagant lifestyles, however, and decline set in. Throughout the 1800s, Russia and Britain fought for control over the Iranian government and outlying Iranian territories, because the country lay between the boundaries of their empires. By 1900 many Iranians supported the idea of national laws in the form of a constitution to curb the shahs' excesses and protect the country from foreign influence. In 1905 demonstrations and strikes forced the shah to submit to a freely elected parliament (the Majlis). Fearing this new independence, Britain financed the exploration for oil in southwest Iran in 1908 and bought a majority share in the country's petroleum industry, while Russia backed royalist attempts to dissolve the elected government.

After World War I, as Britain continued efforts to control the country, a prominent nationalist organized a successful *coup* and declared himself the new shah, renaming himself Reza Shah Pahlavi. The new shah initiated an ambitious modernization scheme, developing industry, infrastructure, and public education, and he sent many Iranians to Europe for training. A professional middle class and a new working class emerged, but the shah's repression of his political enemies increasingly alienated the general population.

 # Words to Understand in This Chapter

autocratic—characteristic of a ruler with unlimited power.

bazaar—an area of small shops and people selling various goods.

coup—a sudden, illegal, often violent seizure of government.

Mahdi—according to Shiite belief, the 12th and last Imam, who has been hidden from humanity's view for centuries but will reappear to usher in a period of justice before Judgment Day.

Marxism—a set of social, political, and economic principles advocated by Karl Marx, including common ownership of means of production.

Mohammad Mosaddeq, a champion of nationalizing Iran's oil industry and a frequent critic of the shah, served as prime minister between 1951 and 1953, when he was ousted by pro-shah forces supported by the U.S. Central Intelligence Agency.

During World War II, after Britain and the Soviet Union became allies, they invaded Iran, sent the shah into exile, and with help from the United States took control of Iran's communication and railroad systems. The shah's son, Mohammad Reza Pahlavi, succeeded him and allowed the parliamentary government to continue, though it had little effective power. In the 1940s reformer Mohammad Mosaddeq campaigned against Western control over Iran's economy and against the shah's dictatorship. He led a highly popular movement to turn the oil industry over to the national government, and in 1951 the Majlis nationalized the oil industry and appointed Mosaddeq prime minister. Britain retaliated with a blockade on Iranian oil exports, which took a devastating toll on the economy. As the Cold War geared up, the United States—perceiving Iran as a key front for preventing Soviet expansion—sent Central Intelligence Agency (CIA) operatives to help overthrow Mosaddeq and restore the shah's power. The United States believed that a weak democracy in Iran might invite Soviet intervention in that country's affairs. Under a new agreement, British, Dutch, French, and U.S. companies each gained a share of Iranian oil profits.

Mohammad Reza Pahlavi with his second wife, Queen Soraya, 1962. The shah did much to modernize his country and improve its educational system, but his ruthless repression of political opponents and his extravagant lifestyle alienated many of his subjects and helped sow the seeds of his downfall.

With the support of his Western allies, the shah established the secret police known as SAVAK to control opposition, and in 1961 he dissolved the Majlis. He continued modernization efforts, but his land reform program did little to help the rural poor, and while his industrial and public works projects did expand the middle class, the migration of poor villagers to the cities in search of jobs led to large slums and degraded living conditions. The shah did not pursue any parallel political reforms; Iran had developed a superior school system, for example, but its well-educated graduates had no real freedom of speech. The shah also gladly accepted military aid from the United States to keep a check on Soviet expansion in the region. When Iran became one of the world's largest exporters of oil, second only to Saudi Arabia, oil revenues provided ample funding for the shah's programs, but the new-found wealth did not trickle down to the middle and working classes.

The Making of a Revolution

Many of the country's intellectuals and professionals attended college in the West and grew concerned about being too dependent on the United States. Meanwhile, religious leaders, the middle-class shop owners of the *bazaars* (*bazaari*), and the working class saw the modernization and the shah's repressive policies as a threat to their religious heritage and national sovereignty. These groups all called for Islamic reforms as key to real change in Iran. However, they did not share the same emphasis on the role of the *ulama* or the same attitudes toward modern practices. The religious and secular groups ultimately had different goals: the religious leaders wanted an emphasis on Islam and an Islamic state, while the others simply wanted to preserve the identity and cultural heritage of Iran and the Shiites.

The country's university students also grew increasingly critical of the shah's *autocratic* rule. Various student groups were repressed by the SAVAK, and many eventually espoused *Marxism* and called for a communist state like that in China or the Soviet Union. The educated middle class was, however, reluctant to participate in a violent struggle. When the Mujahedin-e-Khalq (the People's Combatants) finally attempted an uprising, it did not attract many converts and was brutally put down by the shah's forces.

Ali Shariati (1933–1977), a French-educated writer and lecturer, was a key influence on students and the Mujahedin-e-Khalq. He combined Shiite beliefs and Western science to reinterpret Islam as the religion of the downtrodden—those oppressed by the racist and classist practices of imperialist nations and multinational corporations. He said that waiting on the return of the **Mahdi** (the "Hidden Imam" of Shia tradition, who will reappear before Judgment Day) had made Shiites passive, when they should be actively working to usher in the age of the messiah. This interpretation alarmed both the shah and the *ulama*. Shariati also said that the revolution would start with Iranian intellectuals outside the *ulama*, which resonated with Iran's growing professional class and university groups.

But it was, in fact, the *ulama* who held the key to a successful revolution. They were able to organize and mobilize a broader base of support through their extensive network of mosques and mosque leaders (*mullahs*). Life in the bazaars was built around the mosques and the tombs of Shia saints, which are highly venerated and often visited by Shiites. The mullahs were organized in a tight hierarchy under the elite spiritual authorities known as the ayatollahs. They were also financially independent of the government, unlike the *ulama* in countries dominated by Sunni Muslims. The mullahs collected and redistributed the yearly Muslim tax to benefit the poor (*zakat*), administered the additional Shiite tax on income (*khums*), and ran local schools (*madrassas*). In his hostility toward the mullahs, the shah began to require attendance at modern, state-run schools, a move that infuriated the mullahs and increased the religious devotion of average Iranians. In 1971 the shah founded a state-sanctioned group of religious authorities that he hoped would eventually replace the mullahs.

The mullahs were key to the revolution precisely because Islam was the heart of Iranians' non-Western identity; it provided a common heritage and set of values for all the groups working to overthrow the shah. In addition, the Shiite tradition of opposition was a natural fit for the contemporary situation. Over the centuries, Shiites had come to trace their distinct differences from the Sunnis to the problem of who should have succeeded Muhammad as the leader of the *umma* (the Shiites believed it should have been Muhammad's cousin and son-in-law Ali), and Sunni religious authorities had repeatedly rejected Shiite leaders and put down Shiite rebellions. Shiites also developed a belief in the imminent return of the Mahdi, who would usher in an era of complete social harmony and justice. Thus, the Islamic cry to battle injustice and protect the powerless always rang especially true for the Shiites, and Iranian opposition leaders took it as their own. Mosques in cities and towns across the country became sites for meeting and organizing.

But many of the mullahs were uncertain about the revolutionary ideas espoused by one of their colleagues, the Ayatollah Ruhollah Khomeini (1900/1902–1989). Khomeini had become a hero for the Iranian masses after 1962, when he spoke out publicly against the shah's efforts to modernize Iran. He was taken into custody, which caused mass demonstrations in several cities, and was kept under house arrest until 1964. That year, he again criticized the shah, this time for purchasing American weapons and for granting diplomatic immunity to American military personnel in Iran. The shah forced Khomeini into exile, first in Turkey, then in the Shiite holy city of An Najaf in Iraq, and finally in Paris, the city from which he guided the last stages of the revolution.

From outside Iran, Khomeini could speak without fear of reprisal. He condemned the United States for consciously Westernizing Muslim nations and extending its influence by supporting Israel. He also called for Islam to be implemented on a national level in Iran. He rejected Shariati's claim that the mullahs had been ineffective as advisers to the rulers of Iran, and he went a step further, saying that the country should be ruled by Islamic law and that the most qualified national leaders would be the *ulama* themselves.

Khomeini maintained that the highest power should be given to a cleric well versed in Islamic law (a *faqih*). Many of the mullahs inside Iran understood Khomeini to mean himself, and their leader, the grand ayatollah, publicly opposed the idea. Most of the mullahs also opposed the idea of having too much political power; they preferred to continue operating independently of the government, which they believed by nature to be impure.

The exiled Khomeini became a worldwide symbol of opposition to the shah's oppression, though he was also able to communicate with and guide his followers inside Iran. Cassettes of his speeches and copies of his writings were routinely smuggled into Iran through mosques. But, in spite of his popularity, Khomeini did not emerge as the leader of a broad-based opposition movement in Iran until early 1976.

In 1975 a drop in oil prices led to an economic and social crisis in Iran. The shah responded by halting many business practices of the *bazaari* and throwing some of them in prison, a move that only hardened their opposition. He initiated a similar crackdown on the rest of the middle class.

In 1977 the new U.S. president, Jimmy Carter, demanded that the shah respect human rights by opening up government processes and reining in the SAVAK. The shah began to loosen his stranglehold on the country, but this only increased the opposition's demands. The secular middle class rallied the urban working class,

From exile the Shiite cleric Ayatollah Ruhollah Khomeini, seen here in a 1978 photo, served as the spiritual leader of Iran's Islamic Revolution.

adopting the slogan "Death to the Shah," but this coalition did not have the community base it needed to organize widely. The student groups were also weak, their organization damaged by years of repression.

Khomeini soon became the key figure who would hold the opposition together and increase the levels of protest. In early 1978 a Tehran newspaper published a scathing attack on Khomeini, which united all factions of the resistance in his defense. Even those who did not believe in the concept of a *faqih* were so angered by the attack on Khomeini that they rallied to his side.

Through the mullahs, the entire Iranian network of mosques was at Khomeini's disposal. Without their own ways of reaching the masses, the student groups and middle class united behind Khomeini, too. And Khomeini's charisma did provide coherence: he conveyed a direct message of return to Islam, his simple lifestyle stood in stark contrast to the excesses of the shahs, and his long years of organizing from abroad gave him an army of followers within Iran.

Khomeini's brilliance lay in using Islamic rituals to pull opposition forces together. Every public religious gathering became an occasion for protest: his taped speeches were played during Friday prayers at the mosques, ritual processions became demonstrations in the streets, and the devotional activities of Ramadan were harnessed to further energize the movement. Demonstrators routinely united in shouting *"Allahu Akhbar"* ("God is great"). In addition, rather than launch violent attacks on the shah's military forces, Khomeini prohibited Iranian Shiites from attacking their brothers in the military and invited military personnel to join the cause of the revolution. He also avoided any discussion of the concept of the *faqih*, since he knew this would alienate some sectors of the movement, and he used some of Shariati's terminology to draw in socialist students.

From his exile, Khomeini directed his followers in Iran to incite a series of nationwide strikes and demonstrations. These eventually placed so much pressure on the government that the shah was forced to leave the country in January 1979. Khomeini had developed a network of revolutionary committees based in mosques, and they stepped in to act as police and civil authorities. Within weeks, Khomeini had formed a provisional government, and in a national referendum in March, more than 98 percent of Iranians said yes to an Islamic state.

The controversy over how exactly Iran would be ruled began almost immediately. While most welcomed Khomeini's emphasis on open elections and representative government, secular leaders and some religious leaders opposed the idea of the *faqih*, and minorities like the Kurds and Turkomen argued for greater power for the non-Persian parts of the country. By the end of the year, however, Iran had adopted a constitution that declared Khomeini *faqih* for life and specified a president, a prime minister, a representative Majlis, and a 12-member Council of Guardians, which must approve all laws considered by the Majlis. In contrast to Saudi Arabia, Iran had developed an Islamic state with open processes, including separate legislative, executive, and judicial branches; popular election of the president; and an assembly of experts to be convened to select all subsequent *faqihs*.

After the Revolution

Under Khomeini's leadership, the Islamic Revolutionary Party quickly consolidated its power over the new government, eliminating secular leaders from positions of power. Khomeini himself declared who and what was Islamic, and he eliminated those he deemed un-Islamic from government, military, and educational institutions. He also ruled that Iranian society had to be freed from corrupt practices and thus banned alcohol, gambling, pornography, mixed bathing, and nightclubs. Friday worship became the center of community life, and all Friday prayer leaders were appointed and supervised by Khomeini. The Council of Guardians, made up of six clergy members and six Islamic lawyers, ensured that all legislation passed by the Majlis conformed to Islamic law.

Several significant events hastened the consolidation of Khomeini's power. Militant students seized the U.S. embassy in Tehran in November 1979, ushering in a phase of extreme anti-American sentiment among young Iranians and leading the United States to cut off diplomatic ties with Iran. Iraq invaded Iran in September 1980, as Saddam Hussein called on oil-rich Iranians to resist the new government, but the ensuing war incited patriotism among Iranians that actually benefited Khomeini's regime.

Meanwhile, some Sunni leaders in neighboring countries worried about the ways the Iranian revolution might inspire Muslims in their states. They denounced Shiites as a heretical sect, asserting that Shiites were not true Muslims, and thus attempted to limit the international influence of Iranian revolutionary ideals.

Under Khomeini's leadership, the new Iranian government confiscated the property and wealth of the upper class (now in exile or executed) and nationalized banks and businesses to gain tighter

An anti-U.S. demonstration in Tehran, December 1979. Such scenes were common in the early days of the Islamic Revolution, as the Ayatollah Khomeini labeled the United States "the Great Satan."

control over the economy. But the Council of Guardians, in alliance with the *bazaaris*, repeatedly defeated further restrictions on property rights, and the government found itself putting down rebellions by socialist groups, the only remaining voice of the urban poor.

The Iranian government also faced numerous internal struggles over other issues. In spite of opposition, the Council of Guardians quickly increased the legal list of moral offenses and strictly enforced, for example, an Islamic dress code for women. In addition, though many opposed interfering in the affairs of other peoples and countries, support flowed out of Iran for revolutionary movements in Lebanon, Saudi Arabia, Bahrain, Iraq, and the Philippines. Khomeini also issued a fatwa sentencing British author Salman Rushdie to death on the grounds that his book *The Satanic Verses* was blasphemous, which fed perceptions that Iran wanted to impose its will internationally. And after 1980 Iran developed anti-Western policies on a range of international issues; tensions remained high with the United States over the hostage crisis and with France over France's support of Iraq.

After Khomeini's death in 1989, however, President Hashemi Rafsanjani was able to restrict the power of some of the more conservative members of the Council of Guardians and implement economic reform, and during the 1990s, momentum built among younger Iranians and women for liberal reforms at the national level. In 1997 the country elected Mohammad Khatami president of Iran with over 70 percent of the vote, a result interpreted as a call for more democracy and less power for Khomeini's successor, Ali Khamenei, and the Council of Guardians.

Although Khatami was elected as a moderate reformer, and re-elected in 2001 with another large majority, conservative religious forces in Iran strongly resisted Khatami's policies during his two terms in office. In June 2003, student protests against Iran's powerful Shia clerics rocked Tehran. In the ensuing months, however, reformers found themselves outmaneuvered and marginalized by hard-liners. The Council of Guardians disqualified thousands of reform candidates for the Majlis, leaving conservatives in control of the Iranian parliament after the February 2004 elections. The following year, the extremely conservative former mayor of Tehran, Mahmoud Ahmadinejad, was elected president of Iran.

During the Ahmadinejad era (2006–2013) the Iranian government was accused of supporting international terrorism by Islamic jihadists. Although Sunni jihadists theologically oppose Iran's Shiite majority, they share a common hatred of western influences and, particularly, of the existence of Israel. Iran was also subject to international sanctions due to concerns that it was attempting to develop nuclear weapons.

In 2013, Hassan Rouhani, a reformist cleric, was elected president of Iran. After a long series of negotiations with six world powers, a tentative agreement was announced in April 2015 that would limit Iran's nuclear program. However, many international leaders and political analysts remained leery of Iran's nuclear intentions and its willingness to have its military sites inspected by U.N. officials.

 ## Text-Dependent Questions

1. What US president demanded that the shah do more to protect the human rights of Iranians?
2. What is the Council of Guardians?

 ## Research Project

Using the Internet or your school library, find out more about the events inside Iran during the 1970s that culminated in the overthrow of the shah and the rise to control of Ayatollah Khomeini in 1979. Write a two-page report on the situation inside Iran for your teacher, and present it to the class.

4

Saudi Arabia

Saudi Arabia was established as the first modern Islamic state in 1932, but its origins lie in the Wahhabi movement of the 1700s, when Islamic scholar Muhammad ibn Abd al-Wahhab and tribal chief Muhammad ibn Saud formed an alliance to seek power.

As the location of the holy cities of Mecca and Medina and the site of the annual hajj to Mecca, Saudi Arabia is still very important to Islamic faith and practice. The Saudi royal family and religious leaders claim that Saudi Arabia is the protector of the holy cities and of Muslim pilgrims. They further maintain that, in spite of its great oil wealth and its alliances with Western nations, the kingdom is still true to the tenets of Wahhabism.

Wahhabis and the House of Saud

After legal training in Mecca and Medina, al-Wahhab returned to his hometown of Najd and was appalled to find few Islamic rituals

Opposite: Pilgrims walk around the Kaaba during the hajj, an annual pilgrimage of Muslims to Mecca. Because it contains Islam's holiest sites, Saudi Arabia claims a special position within the Muslim faith. But that status can be a double-edged sword: Islamic militants have criticized the Saudi monarchy for allowing the influence of Westerners in the land of the Prophet's birth.

observed and superstition and tribal conflict rampant. Al-Wahhab thought the moral decay and tribal warfare in Arabia indicated a betrayal of Islam and a breakdown in the *umma*. He blamed the chaos in Arabia on innovations in Islamic practice—especially Sufi practices like the worship of saints and visits to their tombs—and called for a return to the practices of Muhammad and his companions. Al-Wahhab believed that all events after Muhammad's day, including legal rulings of the *ulama*, were open for review and reinterpretation based on the earliest sources of Islam. He advocated the practice of *ijtihad* (individual interpretation of the law) as the only way to rid Islam of the corrupt beliefs and practices he thought were eating away at the fabric of Islamic society.

Al-Wahhab's followers have commonly been called the Wahhabis, though at the time they called themselves the Muwahiddun (the "Unitarians" who proclaim and uphold monotheism). The Wahhabis began to destroy Sufi shrines, tombs, and holy trees, which upset local citizens so much that they drove al-Wahhab's forces out in 1744.

The Wahhabis found refuge in Diriya, where al-Wahhab developed an alliance with the House of Saud through the local tribal chief, Muhammad ibn Saud (d. 1765). They sought to unite devout Muslims under the banner of true Islam and declared holy war on any person, Muslim or otherwise, who did not join their fight. Al-Wahhab provided the spiritual foundation for their struggle, but Saud was declared imam and directed the warfare.

The Wahhabis continued destroying tombs and shrines. In 1802 they massacred the townspeople of Karbala and *desecrated* the tomb of Hussein (the Prophet's grandson), an action for which many Shiites have never forgiven the Wahhabis. By 1805 the

 Words to Understand in This Chapter

apostasy—the renunciation of one's religious or political beliefs.
desecrate—to treat a sacred place or thing with violent disrespect; to violate.

Wahhabis had seized Mecca and Medina, destroying the domes over the graves of Muhammad and his companions. Under Wahhabi rule, Arabian culture changed drastically. The Wahhabis prohibited fancy dress, jewelry, and art forms such as dance and poetry.

However, the Wahhabis' control of Mecca and Medina led to an inevitable conflict with the Ottoman Empire, which saw Wahhabi rule in Arabia as a threat to the stability of the Middle East, and more particularly to the thriving pilgrimage trade in Damascus and Baghdad. Therefore, in 1812 the sultan of the empire sent forces against the Wahhabis. By 1819 the Wahhabis were thoroughly defeated and their imam, Abdullah ibn Saud, was executed. This ended the first phase of Wahhabi rule, but the alliance between the House of Saud and the Wahhabis did not end.

The Founding of Saudi Arabia

After a long period of dormancy, the Saudi dynasty reemerged in 1902, when Abdul Aziz ibn Saud captured the Arabian city Riyadh and began gradually to extend his territory. Most of Ibn Saud's warriors, called the *Ikhwan* ("brotherhood"), were Bedouins. They were fierce in battle, very interested in the loot they could win in war, and confident that if they died fighting they would become martyrs and immediately go to paradise.

Ibn Saud, who saw the Arabian tribes relying on tribal law rather than Islamic law to settle their conflicts, stressed the equality of all Muslims and sought to replace tribal affiliations with loyalty to Islam—a repeat of the intervention in Arab tribal society by Muhammad ibn Saud and Muhammad ibn Abd al-Wahhab. Abdul Aziz ibn Saud asserted his authority as the descendant of both the House of Saud and al-Wahhab—the two families had intermarried extensively since their alliance was first formed more than a century before. Ibn Saud also married into the families of tribal chiefs in order to solidify his control over their tribes.

Under Ibn Saud's direction, the Wahhabis identified, and subjected to dire punishment or even death, any Muslims they deemed to have strayed from the faith by failing to follow Islamic law.

They encouraged nomadic tribes to settle in colonies, where life was organized around the mosque and where they were educated in Wahhabism and observed for correct behavior.

By the early 1920s, Ibn Saud had greatly expanded his territory on the Arabian Peninsula. In 1924 he took control of Mecca, and a year later Medina also surrendered. But Ibn Saud did not completely secure his power over the Arabian Peninsula until 1929, and part of the struggle occurred from within his own ranks. The Ikhwan, now numbering 150,000, were unhappy that Ibn Saud allowed non-Wahhabi pilgrims to the holy sites, maintained a tobacco tax as a way to fill the government's coffers (they considered smoking against Islamic law), and used modern technology. The zeal of the Wahhabis also proved problematic for Ibn Saud; they wanted to move beyond the peninsula to continue to defeat unbelievers and spread Wahhabi beliefs, while he sought to implement fixed national borders and thus gain recognition from foreign powers for his new nation.

With the help of the British, Ibn Saud finally assembled a separate army and defeated the Ikhwan. Thus, the political arm of the Wahhab-Saud alliance won out, and the purely spiritual war waged by the Wahhabis was over. In September 1932, Abdul Aziz ibn Saud declared himself king and named the new nation the Kingdom of Saudi Arabia. While he had thwarted the Wahhabi drive to conquer territory beyond Saudi Arabia, Ibn Saud remained true to the alliance by putting the crossed swords of al-Wahhab and the House of Saud on the country's new flag.

The Enforcement of Islamic Law

Under Ibn Saud, the House of Saud unified the tribal cultures of Arabia and become the first modern Islamic state. Ibn Saud emphasized his role as keeper of the holy cities of Mecca and Medina and as protector of all pilgrims making the annual hajj to Mecca. He assumed power as the head of the government, the commander of the armed forces, and the chief over all Arabian tribes. He also declared that the position of leader would be passed down through his family.

Ibn Saud stipulated the Qur'an as Saudi Arabia's constitution. He said an advisory assembly made up of *ulama* and lay business and community leaders would form to advise him on matters of governance, but he never established this council. In 1960 a new national constitution was proposed to Abdul Aziz ibn Saud's successor, King Saud ibn Saud. It would declare Islam the state religion, affirm the right to private property and capital, and create a national legislative assembly,

Abdul Aziz ibn Saud, founder of the Kingdom of Saudi Arabia.

two-thirds of which would be popularly elected. Saud rejected the proposal, citing the Qur'an as the only constitution Saudi Arabia would ever need.

In 1962, after the Islamic monarch of North Yemen was overthrown in a popular uprising, King Saud and his brother Faisal ibn Saud feared a similar rebellion in Saudi Arabia. To forestall this, they promised economic development and a new constitution based on the Qur'an and the Hadith that would guarantee basic rights to all citizens, including some freedom of expression. They also promised a judicial council to reinterpret the Sharia in light of the problems presented by modern society. The council was not formed until 1975, however, and constitutional reforms finally enacted by King Fahd in 1992 still stipulated the Qur'an and the Hadith as the constitution of Saudi Arabia and did not make any provisions for freedom of speech. A new advisory assembly was also formed in 1992, but the king appointed its members.

The enforcement of Islamic behavior in Saudi Arabia is conducted locally through the mosque leader (imam), the *ulama*, religious judges (*qadi*), and the religious police (*muttawin*). The *muttawin* make sure all citizens comply with Islamic law and practices and provide instruction on how to follow Islamic legal rulings. They see to it that businesses close during prayer times, no one consumes alcohol, and no one breaks the Ramadan ban on food and drink from sunrise to sunset. Worship is also monitored; any speeches given in a mosque must be pre-approved. Women must wear Islamic dress (a loose black cloak called an *abaya* and a headscarf called a *hijab*) while in public, and they can't leave the house alone or drive.

The national minister of religion and justice, traditionally a descendant of al-Wahhab himself, advises the king, as does the chief *qadi*. The judiciary branch is made up entirely of *ulama*, who rely solely on the Sharia. The courts rule on matters of family and property law. The death penalty is mandatory—and usually applied quickly—for adultery, murder, robbery that involves violence, drug violations, and *apostasy*, and it is sometimes decreed for those who exercise freedom of speech.

However, while the *ulama* follow the Hanbali school of Sunni Islamic law and apply it very strictly where specific laws exist, they rule more liberally on other matters. Thus, although women face many restrictions in their daily lives, they are allowed education through the university level, and many hold professional jobs. And while the Wahhabis and some of the *ulama* declared modern technology like phones, cars, airplanes, and television unacceptable Western innovations, the monarchy has persisted and gained acceptance for their use.

Relationship with the World

A dual allegiance to the West and to Arab countries has consistently complicated Saudi Arabia's foreign affairs, a situation created in part by the 1938 discovery of oil in Saudi Arabia under

King Abdul Aziz ibn Saud. From the beginning of oil exploration, American and European technicians and engineers came to work in the kingdom, a fact condemned by Wahhabist leaders.

By 1950 the Arabian-American Oil Company (Aramco) was generating vast wealth from oil sales, primarily in the West. King Saud fostered his country's relationship with the United States, allowing American forces use of an air base in Dhahran and purchasing significant quantities of U.S. arms. The sons of wealthy families were also sent to study at U.S. universities. As interaction with the West increased, however, the *ulama* and the monarchy joined the Wahhabists in worrying about excessive Western influence.

King Saud's half-brother Faisal became king in 1964. He was a pious favorite of the *ulama* who claimed maternal lineage from al-Wahhab. Under King Faisal, the Saudi government refused to renew the U.S. lease on the Dhahran base in 1962. In 1967 Faisal enacted a series of reforms that imposed stricter dress codes for women and children and enforced prayer times for government employees. The king led the 1973–74 Organization of Petroleum Exporting Countries (OPEC) oil embargo on the nations that supported Israel in its 1973 war with Egypt and Syria. The embargo resulted in a spike in worldwide oil prices, and the increased revenues that flowed into Saudi Arabia as a result enabled Faisal to improve his country's transportation, education, and health care systems.

However, Faisal was unwilling to adopt policies that were completely anti-Western. In 1971 Saudi Arabia and five other Persian Gulf countries signed a new agreement with Western oil companies. By the mid-1970s, the number of American civilian and military personnel working in Saudi Arabia had increased dramatically, and many members of the government openly flirted with American values and lifestyles. Wealthy Arab businessmen and princes, it was rumored, engaged in all kinds of Western vices—drinking, gambling, adultery—in their palaces and abroad.

Saudi Arabia has about one-quarter of the world's proven reserves of petroleum. While oil has brought incredible wealth into the kingdom, it has also brought Western influences—a situation condemned by Saudi Arabia's conservative Wahhabi Muslims.

In March 1975, Faisal was assassinated by a nephew and succeeded by Khalid ibn Abdul Aziz. The Saudi government struggled to keep up with the fast pace of development brought on by the oil economy and mass migrations to the cities. The revolution in Iran in 1979 deeply alarmed the monarchy, especially since the Iranian media repeatedly accused the House of Saud of corrupt behavior. King Khalid responded by cracking down on practices that could be considered un-Islamic and publicly punishing royals who broke the law. Then, in late 1979, 400 armed Wahhabist militants, distressed by what they saw as the materialism of the Saudi rulers, seized Islam's holiest shrine, the Grand Mosque in Mecca, and issued demands for changes. Although the government retook the mosque and executed the rebels, this event heightened awareness of the Saudi government's vulnerability to both external and internal threats.

Increasing Fundamentalist Opposition

Khalid died in June 1982 and was succeeded by Fahd, who sought to maintain traditional Islamic values while continuing the process of rapid modernization. He stressed his role as the custodian of Islam's holiest sites to try to shield the pro-West Saudi regime from opposition by Islamic militants. In 1987, however, more than 400 people were killed when Saudi police clashed with Iranian hajj pilgrims. Relations between Saudi Arabia and Iran deteriorated, and Iranian pilgrims boycotted the hajj for several years.

Fundamentalist opposition to the Saudi regime increased through the 1990s. After Iraq invaded Kuwait in 1990, the Saudi government allowed hundreds of thousands of U.S.-led coalition troops to deploy on its territory, which opposition leaders denounced as a violation of sacred Islamic territory. Nevertheless, U.S. forces remained stationed in Saudi Arabia for more than a decade. In 1994 the Saudi government cracked down on fundamentalist clergy and scholars and established the Higher Council for Islamic Affairs to curb fundamentalist tendencies among the *ulama*.

Terrorist incidents on Saudi soil in the 1990s illustrated the level of militant frustration with the Saudi government's ties to the West, and the United States in particular. In 1995 a car bomb killed seven people, including five Americans, at the offices of the Saudi National Guard in Riyadh. In 1996 a bomb exploded at the Khobar Towers housing complex for U.S. military personnel near Dhahran, killing 19 U.S. soldiers and wounding 300 others.

Threats against military personnel were made in subsequent years, and in 2003, as the U.S. military was pulling out of the country, three foreign residential compounds in Riyadh were hit by suicide bombings, killing 35. Among the dead were Americans, Europeans, and Saudis; it was the first time terrorists had target-ed civilians, including women and children, in Saudi Arabia.

Critics of close U.S.-Saudi relations point to the fact that, though the Saudi government has officially denounced terrorism, many Saudi individuals and charities have used the kingdom's great wealth to spread Wahhabi-style fundamentalist thought throughout the Islamic world. By gaining extensive control of printing presses in the Middle East, these fundamentalists have ensured a pro-Wahhabi bent in publications, and they have estab-lished schools and mosques throughout the Islamic world to teach

The ruins of the Khobar Towers housing complex near Dhahran, Saudi Arabia, where in 1996 a truck bomb claimed the lives of 19 U.S. Air Force personnel. The United States later indicted 14 members of the militant Islamic organization Hizbollah in the attack; 13 were Saudis.

fundamentalist Wahhabi doctrine. Today, Saudi individuals and charities routinely fund militant groups in Syria, Iraq, Yemen, the Philippines, Chechnya, the Balkans, Egypt, and Somalia, among other places. Links have also been alleged between Saudi sources and the terrorist organizations Hamas and al-Qaeda.

A Strict Legal System

The strict Wahhabi version of Sharia applies to all areas of life in Saudi Arabia. Because Sharia requires modesty, there is a rigid standard of dress, particularly for women. The law requires women to cover their bodies when they are in public. Women must wear long, flowing gowns. The gowns, known as *abayahs*, must be solid black, with no decorations. They cover the entire body, including the face, from head to toe. They conceal so much, in fact, that it is impossible for an observer to tell whether a woman beneath an *abayah* is young or old, thin or plump. Even in the heat of summer, all women must wear the thick, black gowns.

The law concerning *abayahs* is taken quite seriously. In January 2015, the government formally ordered female news readers on Saudi television stations to wear *abayahs*. The mandate was in response to an incident in which a Saudi journalist broadcasting from London wore no head covering. Other laws governing dress and conduct are treated with equal seriousness.

Islamic law is enforced in Saudi Arabia by a special group known as the Committees for the Propagation of Virtue and the Prevention of Vice. The committee agents are called the Mutawin. Their headquarters is in an office in Riyadh called the Royal Diwan, where the king also has his own headquarters.

The Mutawin have been part of the Wahhabi movement since its beginnings. In the early 1800s, the Mutawin acted as a form of religious police, physically forcing men to join in public prayer. Today, the Mutawin continue to enforce moral standards in Saudi Arabia. Their findings are taken quite seriously.

In 1991, for example, the Mutawin caught a Saudi man giving

When Saudi Arabia's King Abdullah died at age 90 in January 2015, he was succeeded by Salman bin Abd al-Aziz Al Saud, his 79-year-old half brother. King Salman (left) is pictured meeting with US Secretary of State John Kerry in 2015.

a female coworker a ride home from work. The act was forbidden; men and women who are not married or are not close relatives cannot be alone together. The woman, who came from a different country, was ordered to return to her native land. The man was beaten in public.

Punishments for other offenses are also harsh by Western standards. Thieves who are repeatedly caught stealing can have their right hands chopped off. People convicted of crimes related to alcohol can be whipped with a cane.

One of the most far-reaching set of laws in Saudi Arabia is that governing religious practice. All citizens must follow the teachings of Islam. The government is vigilant at keeping the country free of non-Muslim influences. Government inspectors routinely open mail from foreign countries and search for such items as Bibles or non-Islamic religious videos.

Theoretically, non-Muslims are allowed to practice their faiths in private, but no one is entirely sure what that means. In recent years, the U.S. State Department has reported several cases where non-Muslims have been punished for attending private religious services. In one instance, 16 Filipinos were arrested for attending a Christian prayer service. The Filipinos were later sent back to the Philippines. The State Department also reported that, an elderly man was attacked and killed because he performed a Shiite Muslim ritual in public.

Wahhabi leaders in Saudi Arabia generally denounce Shiite Muslims as apostates who have fallen away from the true path of Islam. Shiites in Saudi Arabia make up 10 to 15 percent of the kingdom's population, but they generally face discrimination in education and in the workplace. No Shia Muslims hold high-ranking positions in the Saudi government or military. Worse, Shiites are often the target of violence, particularly those who are participating in pilgrimages to the shrines of Shia imams or saints. Shiites who have protested against the repressive government policies have been arrested on charges that include terrorism; some have been executed. Such actions have been criticized by the Shiite leadership of Iran, Saudi Arabia's greatest rival for regional influence. In January 2016, tensions between the two countries rose after King Salman ordered the execution of a Shiite cleric, Nimr al-Nimr, along with 46 other dissidents.

 # Text-Dependent Questions

1. What Saudi king was assassinated in 1975?
2. What group enforces religious law in Saudi Arabia?

 # Research Project

Saudi Arabia is said to be the only nation in the world that forbids women from driving. Examine the issue historically and through recent events. Write a report on the current status of the push for women's rights in Saudi Arabia.

5

The Arab World

The Arab world includes areas of both the Middle East and North Africa. Most Arabs do have considerable linguistic and cultural connection to the peoples of Arabia, but some are considered Arab only because their lands were conquered during eras of Arab expansion. Arab countries in the Middle East include Bahrain, Iraq, Jordan, Kuwait, Lebanon, Oman, Qatar, Saudi Arabia, Syria, the United Arab Emirates, and Yemen. Arab countries in North Africa include Algeria, Djibouti, Egypt, Libya, Mauritania, Morocco, Somalia, Sudan, and Tunisia.

Islamic fundamentalism has deep roots in the Arab region. The predominantly Muslim countries of the region have been at the center of conflict between the Islamic and secular modern worldviews for several reasons: the central Middle East was the site of some of the greatest Western colonial expansion, the West backed the founding of Israel, and colonialism and its aftermath brought severe economic

Opposite: A Turkish soldier patrols the fence around a refugee camp for Syrians fleeing from the violent civil war in their country. Conflict in Syria, Iraq, Libya, and other Arab countries, fueled in part by Islamist parties like the Islamic State of Iraq and the Levant (ISIL) has contributed to the greatest humanitarian crisis since the end of World War II. In 2016 there were more than 60 million refugees worldwide.

and educational impoverishment and brutal political repression to the region. As Arab countries have experienced rapid change and severe social problems, many Muslims have found a renewed sense of identity by returning to their faith.

Together with a Pan-Arab consciousness, which promotes the interests of Arabs in general, Islamic fundamentalism has dominated political life in the Arab world since the late 1800s. Since the 1970s, however, as secular nationalism has faltered, Islamic fundamentalism has increasingly replaced the Pan-Arab movement by promising to cleanse the region of foreign influences and provide political and economic stability through the application of Islamic principles.

Two central factors, the birth of Israel and the discovery of oil, have shaped the history of the Arab world in the last century. *Ideological* and military conflicts over these two developments opened the way for fundamentalism to grow in strength and influence.

Opposition to Israel

Arab solidarity would be seriously tested, and relations with Western powers severely strained, in the aftermath of the creation of Israel in 1948. Nearly 70 years later, Israel (along with the plight of Palestinians under the control of the Jewish state) remains a major concern for Islamic fundamentalists in the Arab world.

 Words to Understand in This Chapter

Druze—a Middle Eastern religion characterized by monotheism and a belief in al-Hakim (985–1021) as the embodiment of God.

ideological—relating to the beliefs on which an organization or political system is based.

indigenous—originating in a place rather than arriving from another place.

intifada—an uprising against Israeli rule among Palestinians of the Gaza Strip and West Bank.

On May 14, 1948, when Britain officially withdrew from Palestine and Israel declared its independence, the armies of Arab League members Egypt, Transjordan (later Jordan), Iraq, Syria, and Lebanon, as promised, moved to crush the new Jewish state. In the ensuing war, however, Israel not only defeated all its Arab enemies but also gained significantly more territory than had been allotted it under the U.N. partition plan. For the Palestinians, the war was a catastrophe. By the time the fighting ended in January 1949, about 750,000 had been uprooted from their homes, and the Palestinian state envisioned in the U.N. partition plan was gone. Israel had conquered some of the territory; Egypt had taken Gaza, along the Mediterranean coast; and Jordan occupied the West Bank.

Over the following decades, Arab-Israeli relations remained abysmal. The Arab countries refused to recognize Israel's right to exist, and skirmishes between Israel and its neighbors erupted periodically. In 1956 Israel defeated Egypt during the Suez War, capturing most of the Sinai Peninsula but later returning the territory at the insistence of the United States. Following an Arab conference in Cairo, Egypt, in 1964, the Palestine Liberation Organization (PLO) was formed. Its mission was to unify Palestinian efforts to "liberate" Palestine from Israel, and funding came from various Arab governments.

The Six-Day War, fought in June 1967, was a watershed in the Arab-Israeli conflict. As Egypt, Syria, and Jordan were preparing to attack the Jewish state, Israel struck first. In less than a week, Israel smashed the combined armed forces of its enemies. The decisive defeat struck a devastating blow to Arab confidence; Israel clearly was the region's preeminent military power. (Arab critics charged that this was due largely to the military aid Israel received from the West, especially the United States.) As a result of the Six-Day War, Israel also took control of additional territory: Gaza and most of the Sinai Peninsula, which had belonged to Egypt; Syria's Golan Heights; and the West Bank, which Jordan had claimed since 1948. Most significantly, this brought several million Palestinians in Gaza and the West Bank under Israeli military occupation, a situation that, over the following decades, would breed more Palestinian and Arab resentment and lead to much bloodshed.

After another war with Israel in October 1973, Egyptian president Anwar Sadat traveled to Jerusalem in 1977 to address Israel's parliament, the Knesset. Sadat announced his desire for peace, and that opening led to the Camp David Accords of 1978, a framework for peace negotiated with mediation from U.S. president Jimmy Carter. The following year, Israel and Egypt concluded an official peace treaty. Under the terms of the treaty Egypt officially recognized Israel, becoming the first Arab nation to do so, and Israel returned the Sinai Peninsula to Egypt.

Sadat's peace agreement with Israel provoked outrage throughout the Arab world, leading to Egypt's expulsion from the Arab League. And, although the Camp David Accords had envisioned a peaceful settlement to the Israeli-Palestinian conflict that might include an independent Palestinian state in the West Bank and Gaza, neither the Arab nations nor the PLO supported such a course. Palestinian grievances against Israel—including ongoing Jewish settlement of the West Bank and Gaza Strip—continued to fester, and in December 1987 a violent Palestinian uprising known as the *intifada* ("shaking off") broke out in the occupied territories.

After several years of almost daily bloodshed, Israel and the PLO began conducting secret negotiations, which culminated in 1993 in the Oslo Accords. That agreement, essentially a land-for-peace deal, called for an Israeli military pullback from most of the occupied territories, a five-year period of security cooperation and limited Palestinian self-rule, and then final-status negotiations to settle outstanding issues and fix the borders of the Palestinian state.

The Oslo Accords paved the way for an Israel-Jordan peace treaty, as well as better Israeli relations with such Arab countries as Qatar, Morocco, and Tunisia. Unfortunately, although a Palestinian governing authority was set up in the West Bank and Gaza under the leadership of PLO chairman Yasir Arafat, the peace process unraveled well before the final-status talks the Oslo Accords had envisioned. A second *intifada*, which broke out in September 2000, effectively ended the Oslo Accords and ushered in a long cycle of Palestinian terrorism and Israeli retaliation.

In August 2005, Israel unilaterally withdrew from its settlements in the Gaza Strip, and dismantled four settlements in the West Bank. However, Israel also moved toward annexing about one-third of the remaining West Bank territory.

In the following years, the militant party Hamas gained control over the Gaza Strip, which it used to launch rocket and mortar attacks against Israel. The country responded with airstrikes and military incursions of its own. In 2006 Israel attacked Lebanon, after a militia affiliated with the Lebanese Islamist party Hezbollah ambushed Israeli soldiers near the border. The Second Lebanon War claimed the lives of more than 1,000 Lebanese, most of them civilians. Israel officially reported 121 of its soldiers killed in action, with more than 40 Israeli civilians also losing their lives. Over the next decade, the pattern of rocket attacks from Gaza and Lebanon, followed by Israeli military responses, would continue.

An Israeli army convoy rolls across Egypt's Sinai Peninsula during the Six-Day War. The June 1967 conflict brought Israel a stunning military victory and important territorial gains—along with the quandary of how to govern several million Palestinians now under its control.

Following elections in February 2009, Likud's Benjamin Netanyahu gained power as Israel's prime minister. Netanyahu would take a hard line on security issues, bringing the Israeli-Palestinian peace process to a virtual standstill. Tensions between the two sides occasionally boiled over into full-fledged conflict, such as in July 2014, when Israel began a massive bombing campaign targeting the Gaza Strip. A week later, Israeli ground forces entered Gaza. By the time the war ended on August 26, 66 Israeli soldiers, along with six Israeli civilians, had been killed. Meanwhile, according to the UN Office for the Coordination of Humanitarian Affairs, some 2,220 Palestinians had lost their lives—and nearly 1,500 of them were civilians. Israel was widely condemned for its failure to take steps to protect noncombatants.

As the peace process has stagnated, Arabs have charged that the United States blindly supports Israel and what they view as its oppression of the Palestinian people. Israel and the United States, in turn, accuse Palestinian leaders of doing nothing to stop suicide

The Camp David Accords marked the first time an Arab nation had made peace with Israel. Seen here celebrating the breakthrough are (from left) President Anwar Sadat of Egypt; U.S. president Jimmy Carter, who helped mediate the agreement; and Menachem Begin, prime minister of Israel.

bombings and rocket attacks targeting Israelis by Arab-supported fundamentalist groups such as Hamas and Islamic Jihad, as well as the Shiite organization Hezbollah. Though statehood for the Palestinians remains a central goal of many Arabs and Islamic fundamentalists, when—or even if—that goal might be achieved remains uncertain.

The Role of Oil

The second major factor that has shaped the contemporary Arab world, after Israel, is oil. Together with Iran, the Middle East has about two-thirds of the world's total known petroleum reserves; Saudi Arabia alone claims about one-quarter of all proven reserves.

The Arab oil-producing states formed the Organization of Petroleum Exporting Countries (OPEC) in 1960. In support of Egypt in the 1973 October War with Israel, OPEC instituted steep price hikes for its crude oil, which further raised U.S. concerns about the security of the oil supply. Since then, U.S. strategists have sought to build a troop presence in the Persian Gulf to ensure the flow of oil in the region. American troops were called into action in the Persian Gulf twice over a dozen-year period. In the Gulf War of 1991, the United States led an international coalition that expelled Iraq from Kuwait, which Iraq had invaded the previous year. In 2003 U.S. forces invaded Iraq and toppled the regime of Saddam Hussein, an action President George W. Bush framed as part of the U.S. "war on terror"; Iraq was said to possess chemical and biological weapons in violation of its obligations under the Gulf War armistice agreement.

In each conflict with Iraq, however, Arab critics (both fundamentalists and others) complained that the main U.S. interest was to protect the flow of oil to American consumers. They condemned U.S. protection of oil resources in the Middle East as Western imperialism, and some even asserted that the United States manufactured both conflicts as pretexts for gaining more control over

Arab oil fields. After the Gulf War of 1991, the United Nations imposed economic sanctions on Iraq in order to compel Saddam Hussein to comply with disarmament obligations. Those sanctions remained in effect for more than a decade, and during that time ordinary Iraqis suffered substantial increases in poverty, illness, and child mortality rates. Many Arabs charged that the United States, the staunchest backer of the sanctions, was interested only in keeping its oil supply secure and did not care about Muslim lives. Further evidence of this, the critics charged, was the slowness with which the United States responded to Serbian atrocities against Muslims during the war in Bosnia in the early 1990s.

Nationalists and Fundamentalists

The birth of Israel in 1948 inspired the growth of Arab nationalism. Radical army officers took over Egypt, Iraq, and Syria and vowed to destroy Israel, maintain independence from foreign influence, and develop strong economies. Though they accepted aid primarily from the Soviet Union, they sought complete sovereignty, established Western-style political patterns (parliaments, political parties, constitutions), and adopted Western legal codes. They attempted to develop modern industrial economies using the latest agricultural, transportation, and communication methods. They also accepted Western styles of art, music, and literature and Western ideas about women's rights.

However, these governments concentrated on military defense and often badly mismanaged resources. Meanwhile, migration to urban centers grew as people looked for jobs, and the gap between the rich and poor increased. The result was unrest and increasingly repressive government policies. The monarchies of Jordan and Saudi Arabia adopted similarly repressive measures to stifle calls for change in their own countries.

Radical nationalism reached its zenith in the 1960s, when Egyptian president Gamal Abdel Nasser and the Baath Party leaders of Iraq and Syria advocated Arab revolutions and social-

Palestinian Arabs carry Palestinian flags during a protest on the Gaza-Israel border. Due to Israel's withdrawal from Gaza, it has become a de facto Palestinian state.

ism. However, military defeats at the hands of Israel and the 1991 collapse of the Soviet Union dealt serious blows to Arab nationalism.

It is no accident that Islamic fundamentalism in the Arab world surged precisely as nationalism began to founder, for it was by pointing both within (at the failures of nationalism and the un-Islamic ways of government leaders) and without (at the corrupting influence of foreign powers) that fundamentalist leaders persuaded Muslims to return to the fundamentals of their faith. This has resulted in opposition movements in numerous Arab countries, including Egypt, Lebanon, and Syria. It has also influenced leaders who had previously relied on secular nationalism alone to embrace Islamic principles in an effort to

A fragment of a rocket that damaged a house in Kfar Aza, Israel. Since Israel withdrew from the Gaza Strip in 2005, terrorists have fired more than 11,000 rockets into Israel. Over 5 million Israelis are currently living under threat of rocket attacks, which cause widespread psychological trauma and disruption of daily life.

boost their legitimacy, as has been the case in Egypt, Iraq, Libya, Sudan, and Syria.

An important turning point was the 1967 Six-Day War with Israel. For Arabs the rapid and total defeat of the combined forces of Egypt, Syria, and Jordan was made even worse because the Israelis captured East Jerusalem and made the unified city their capital. The third-holiest city in Islam, Jerusalem plays an important role in Muslim identity. The Six-Day War starkly illustrated the flaws in the nationalist policies of Arab countries, and particularly the Egyptian brand of socialism. Arab Muslims had won the end of colonial rule, but their societies were caught in a downward spiral of decline. In response, fundamentalists cited the glorious early expansion under Muhammad and the growth of Islamic empires to illustrate that Muslim prosperity depended on being faithful to God in all matters. The current state of affairs in the Arab world, they argued, was the sign of Muslims' disobedience.

This call for religious reform tapped into new sources of pride after Egypt used Islamic symbols and language to motivate its forces to win some battles against Israel in the 1973 October War and OPEC staged its oil embargo later that year. These successes underlined the fundamentalists' message that faithfulness to God would bring new prosperity to Muslim nations. In turn, the wealthy oil nations pumped their petrodollars into Islamic organizations and movements. Finally, though it occurred in a non-Arab country, the Iranian revolution of 1979 further strengthened the claim that following the straight path of Islam would invigorate Muslim movements and lead to freedom from foreign domination.

The fundamentalist response has taken many forms to influence Arab governments in the last 30 years. Most Arab countries have an ongoing fundamentalist presence. In Egypt, Jordan, Lebanon, Kuwait, and Yemen, fundamentalist organizations have run educational and social programs, developed opposition political parties, and even occupied government positions. But militant groups have also proliferated throughout the Arab world, opposing leaders they see as un-Islamic and in turn being repressed by the government. In the Arab-Israeli conflict, the group Hamas has become a major critic of the secular Palestinian Authority.

Fundamentalism in Egypt

Egypt's story can be told through the relationship between three different national governments and a diverse set of moderate and militant fundamentalist groups.

After Gamal Abdel Nasser became president in 1952, he kept Egypt on its secular nationalist path, ignoring the Muslim Brotherhood. Within just a few years, however, their opposition led him to incorporate Islamic symbols and language into his Pan-Arab socialist message in order to gain legitimacy in Islamic terms.

But the Brotherhood saw Nasser's use of Islam as antithetical to a true Islamic state. After extremist members of the Brotherhood led an assassination attempt on Nasser in 1954, he brutally suppressed the organization. A second attempt by Muslim Brothers to overthrow the Nasser regime in 1965 led to the execution of Sayyid Qutb that same year.

After Nasser's death in 1970, President Anwar Sadat began to enact more pro-Western policies. He built mosques and used Islamic symbols and language to bolster his political authority. In spite of Egypt's successes against Israel in the 1973 October War, Sadat moved even closer to the West by participating in the Camp David Accords and supporting the shah of Iran. In order to create a counterweight to Nasserists and leftists, Sadat allowed the Muslim Brotherhood to re-form. Soon, however, the Brotherhood turned against Sadat. Joined by new student groups, the Brotherhood publicly criticized Sadat's relations with the United States and Egypt's peace treaty with Israel.

More radical groups also appeared. Some, founded by former members of the Muslim Brotherhood, believed that Brotherhood leaders had grown lax in their condemnation of Sadat. They accused Sadat of cynically using Islam for political purposes, and

Like his predecessors Anwar Sadat and Gamal Abdel Nasser, Egyptian president Hosni Mubarak resorted to harsh measures to suppress Islamic fundamentalists.

they believed Egypt's leaders were tools of foreign domination. These groups called for the violent overthrow of the government. They also wanted to eliminate Western cultural influences, and among their targets for attack were nightclubs and tourist hotels.

As militant groups increasingly called for armed struggle against Egyptian leaders, Sadat insisted that religion and politics must remain separate. In 1981 he ordered a crackdown in which more than 1,500 Egyptians were jailed for opposition activities. Later that year, members of the militant group Tanzim al-Jihad ("Jihad Organization") assassinated the Egyptian president, claiming his pro-West policies made him a corrupt "pharaoh."

When Hosni Mubarak succeeded Sadat as president, he created a more open atmosphere. He quickly put down militant actions, but he also allowed a measure of free speech in media outlets, and a number of fundamentalist leaders thus gained a wider audience. Fundamentalists began to develop a broader base, fostering renewed religious practices and offering social services in areas like education, banking, and housing.

By the late 1980s, however, Egyptians' increased involvement in Islamic organizations and the government's inability to create economic opportunities for its citizens led to renewed volatility. Mubarak was unhappy with the broad fundamentalist effect on the population. Militant groups assassinated government officials and attacked foreigners, and by the 1990s Mubarak increasingly used authoritarian tactics to suppress all fundamentalist groups, including both the Muslim Brotherhood and the militants. The Brotherhood had become the main opposition in parliamentary elections, but Mubarak shut down their resistance by jailing their key leaders. He also took control of all independent mosques, many of which had been highly critical of his government.

In late 2010 and early 2011, anti-government protests began to occur in a number of Arab countries, beginning with Egypt's North African neighbor Tunisia. The protests—which became known as the "Arab Spring"—were aimed at improving the political circumstances and living conditions of the Arab people. In

Anti-government protesters gathered in Cairo's Tahrir Square, February 2011.

January 2011, Egyptians began to hold mass demonstrations aimed at removing Mubarak from power. The Muslim Brotherhood and other Egyptian Islamist parties played a key role in these protests. By January 29, it was clear that Mubarak's government had lost control, and the Egyptian army declared it would not intervene to stop the protests.

Mubarak attempted to disarm the protests by first firing his top ministers. He later promised not to run in elections scheduled for September. When these steps did not appease the protesters, he resigned as president on February 11, 2011, and fled the country. Commanders of the Egyptian military soon announced that the constitution and the parliament of Egypt had been dissolved, and that new elections would be held later in the year. The military ruled for six months, until parliamentary elections could be held. The Muslim Brotherhood gained a majority of seats in the new parliament, and six months after that, in June 2012, Muslim Brotherhood candidate Mohamed Morsi was elected president.

However, the Muslim Brotherhood and the military soon clashed over control of the country. Morsi oversaw the drafting of a new constitution in 2012. However, he was criticized for trying to extend his powers as president, and some Egyptians became disillusioned since his government did not seem to be as democratic as they had hoped. By June 2013, many Egyptians were demonstrating in the streets again, this time calling for Morsi to be removed from office. The military removed Morsi the following month in a coup d'état led by General Abdel Fattah el-Sisi. Adly Mansour, a judge, became Egypt's interim president, but it was clear that Sisi and the military were running the country. Morsi's supporters protested his removal, but the military cracked down on dissent. Eventually, the military-backed interim government banned the Muslim Brotherhood.

Syria

Egypt was not the only country to experience political turmoil due to the Arab Spring protests. In Syria, the first sign of the Arab Spring was the appearance of graffiti in the city of Daraa that criticized the regime of Bashar al-Assad. The Syrian government responded by arresting the students who were responsible. This led to larger protests. Inspired by successful revolutions in Tunisia and Egypt, Syrian protesters used marches, hunger strikes, rioting, vandalism, and guerrilla attacks to destabilize the Assad regime. The Syrian police and military used force in an effort to quell the demonstrations, but despite the deaths of several people the unrest soon spread throughout the country.

By August 2011, the protests had turned into a violent uprising, with the United Nations and many countries condemning the Syrian government's use of heavy weaponry against rebel forces, as well as the killing of civilians. Several countries, including the United States and Turkey, began to arm and train rebel groups,

A tank belonging to a rebel faction in the Syrian civil war rolls through a street on the outskirts of Damascus, 2013.

while militant Islamist groups in places like Iraq and Libya began to send fighters to Syria.

In June 2012, the Free Syrian Army gained control over most of Aleppo, as well as several other cities and towns in Syria. That rebel group was formed of former Syrian Army officers and soldiers, and trained and supplied by Turkey and the U.S. In November, representatives of the Free Syrian Army met with leaders of other rebel groups in Qatar, where they agreed to form the National Coalition for Syrian Revolutionary and Opposition Forces. (For the most part, Islamist groups fighting in Syria refused to join the Coalition, however.)

The United States, Turkey, Great Britain, France, and more than 120 other countries soon granted official recognition to the

National Coalition as the legitimate representative of the Syrian people. This added another element of international pressure to the regime, which was already dealing with economic sanctions imposed by the Arab League, the European Union, Turkey, and the United States. Beginning in 2012, the United Nations and Arab League sent several special envoys to meet with government leaders in the region and try to resolve the Syrian crisis.

The year 2013 saw the rise of the Islamic State of Iraq and the Levant (ISIL), which was able to capture and hold territory in both Iraq and Syria. That same year, the Assad government was accused of introducing chemical weapons into the civil war. This led to renewed demands for Bashar al-Assad to relinquish power, as well as a threat by U.S. President Barack Obama to consider military options within Syria to remove the Assad regime. Under international pressure, the Syrian government agreed to destroy its chemical weapons through a U.N.-supervised process.

During 2014, the United Nations began holding peace negotiations between the Assad regime and rebel groups. However, the talks went nowhere as Bashar al-Assad refused to step down and turn over power to a transitional government. The Syrian military instead used the cease-fire to prepare for new offensives against rebel positions in Aleppo and elsewhere.

By June 2014, after conquering the city of Mosul in Iraq, ISIL declared itself to be the restoration of the Islamic caliphate. ISIL's extremist leaders claimed that all Muslims needed to swear allegiance to their organization and follow its dictates, and that Islam needed to be returned to a "pure" state by eliminating apostates, or those who do not follow their teachings. ISIL attempted to do this in the territories it controlled by murdering Christians, Jews, Kurds, Shiite Muslims, Druze, and others living in the regions it controlled.

The reports of ISIL atrocities led the United States, Russia, Turkey, France and other countries to intervene in the Syrian civil war with military force. Airstrikes were launched against ISIL positions, although the U.S. and other countries decided not to send in soldiers to wage ground combat.

By 2016, according to the United Nations, more than 220,000 people had been killed in the Syrian civil war, while more than 9 million Syrians—roughly half of the population—were refugees. Syrian civilians have suffered greatly during the war. A UN study found that both sides had engaged in acts that would be considered war crimes—rape, murder, and torture. The Assad regime has used "barrel bombs"—improvised explosive devices dropped from aircraft —to devastate both civilian and rebel populations and turn Syria's once-proud cities into rubble. Tragically, it appears this conflict will not end any time soon.

One of ISIL's stated goals is to bring about a clash with the non-Muslim world, which according to its beliefs the Muslims are destined to win. ISIL's atrocities against Christians and westerners

Belgian soldiers on patrol in European Parliament zone of Brussels, March 2016. Terrorist bombings at the international airport of Brussels, and at a train station, killed more than 30 people and injured over 200 on March 22, 2016. The organization ISIL took credit for the attacks.

has been devoted to this end, along with its destruction of ancient historical sites in Syria and other lands it rules. The group has destroyed Shiite mosques and shrines in Iraq, as well as Christian churches and monasteries. The group has also destroyed ancient ruins, including a pagan temple and a Roman theater in Palmyra, Syria, and structures built during the Assyrian period that date back more than 2,500 years.

ISIL has also attempted to attack the West directly, in hopes of inciting an invasion by ground troops in response. In 2015 and 2016, members of the group carried out terrorist attacks in many countries outside of Iraq and Syria, including a mass shooting at a Tunisian resort, several bombings in Turkey and Lebanon, and the destruction of a Russian airliner carrying 224 people. The November 2015 Paris attacks killed 130 people, while a March 2016 bombing in Brussels, Belgium, killed more than 30 civilians.

 Text-Dependent Questions

1. What event occurred in 1978 that angered many Arab Muslims?

2. Why were many Egyptian Islamists unhappy with the Mubarak regime?

3. What ISIL activities caused western countries like the United States and Russia to launch airstrikes against this faction in the Syrian civil war?

 Research Project

In Islam, a caliphate is a theocratic state in which the ruler (known as a caliph), has authority over both the spiritual and temporal lives of his subjects and all people must obey Islamic laws. The organization ISIL has declared that it is forming a new caliphate, to which all Muslims must pledge allegiance. Find a world map online, and identify the ten countries with the greatest population of Muslims (Indonesia, Pakistan, India, Bangladesh, Egypt, Nigeria, Iran, Turkey, Algeria, and Morocco. How close are these countries to the lands where ISIL holds territory (Iraq and Syria)?

6

Asia

Indonesia is the largest Muslim country in the world, followed by Pakistan, India, and Bangladesh. There are, in fact, many more non-Arab Muslims than Arab Muslims in the world; Indonesia's Muslim population of more than 206 million outnumbers all Arab Muslim populations combined. Correspondingly, while most Islamic fundamentalist thinking has its roots in Arab regions, fundamentalist movements in Southeast Asia, both moderate and militant, have significantly influenced the larger Muslim world and the way non-Muslims view Islamic fundamentalism. Militant movements in particular have taken shape in recent decades, most of them with some connection to militant training centers in Pakistan.

Pakistan

Founded as a country for Muslims in 1947, Pakistan has from the beginning been home to different forms of Islamic fundamentalism.

Opposite: Indonesian Muslim youths perform traditional music. Nearly 9 in 10 Indonesians are followers of Islam, and in recent years the secular government has faced increasing challenges from fundamentalists who wish to make the Southeast Asian nation an Islamic state.

79

Fundamentalists have played a central role in struggles over the relationship between Islam and politics, in training Islamic extremists to fight in Afghanistan and Kashmir, and in sectarian fighting between Sunnis and Shiites.

In the wake of British colonialism, the modernist Mohammed Ali Jinnah and the Muslim League argued that the Muslims and Hindus of India were in fact two separate nations, which led to the birth of Pakistan in 1947. Jinnah saw Islam as simply the common point of identity for Muslims and envisioned a secular country, but Pakistanis have never completely agreed on the question of whether Pakistan should be a state in which Muslims can practice their religion freely or an Islamic state relying on religious institutions and enforcing the Sharia. This tension is clear in the country's constitution, finalized in 1956, which provides for a parliamentary democracy but also calls the state the Islamic Republic of Pakistan and requires that the head of state be a Muslim.

The country's leaders have alternately moved toward and retreated from state-sponsored Islamic law and institutions. Pakistani leaders have routinely used Islamic symbols and language to bolster their authority and policies, which has in turn strengthened the fundamentalist opposition. Fundamentalist groups like the Islamic Society have developed political parties and won some power through parliamentary elections, but most have operated outside the government as a force of resistance. The fundamentalists' influence has in many ways exceeded their relatively small numbers, which many attribute to the fact that Islam is

 Words to Understand in This Chapter

burqa—a robe for women that covers the body from head to toe, with only a grid over the eyes through which to see.

infidels—a person who does not believe in religion or who adheres to a religion other than one's own.

the only common factor of identity for virtually all Pakistanis.

In contrast to the political parties, the Deobandis, a minority Sunni Muslim group in Pakistan whose teachings are similar to those of the Wahhabis, have fueled a more radical Islamic approach. The Deobandis originally formed in India in the mid-1800s, when a group deeply opposed to British rule gathered in the town of Deoband and founded schools for strict Muslim education of boys (*madrassas*). Some Deobandis moved to Pakistan in 1947, where they adopted a more radical stance, arguing against Western imperialism and opposing all forms of Western technology.

These neo-Deobandis founded *madrassas* for Afghan refugees in the vicinity of Peshawar in the Northwest Frontier Province. Many of the *madrassas* were run with Saudi Arabian funding (as a major financial supporter, Osama bin Laden visited Peshawar on numerous occasions), which brought with them a Wahhabi influence. The *madrassas* taught a rigid, militant worldview in which all unbelievers are considered **infidels** and open to attack. By 2001 there were 4,000 Deobandi *madrassas* in Pakistan.

The United States funneled money into Pakistan to train Islamic militants to fight in Afghanistan in the 1980s, and Pakistani agents trained the more promising *madrassa* students (*taliban*) at secret army camps. In 1996 it was *taliban* from Pakistan who formed the Taliban government in Afghanistan. Pakistani prime minister Benazir Bhutto supported the Taliban to prevent Afghanistan from being taken over by a pro-Indian government.

Pakistan has also trained militants to fight in the Kashmiri independence struggle against India, in which 30,000 have died since the late 1980s. Demanding that Kashmir be united with Pakistan and calling for the imposition of the Sharia, Pakistani militants have attracted scores of young Kashmiris to the cause.

To complicate the situation in Pakistan even further, Sunni and Shia Muslims are clashing there in increasingly violent ways. Historical tension between the two sects existed in India, especially when the British pitted the two groups against each other, but

Pakistanis demonstrate in Hyderabad against the US drone program, which is meant to target terrorists but has resulted in civilian casualties at times.

the conflict subsided in the early years of Pakistan's history. After the 1979 Iranian revolution, however, Iran helped the Pakistani Shiites organize a political party, while Saudi Arabia helped create militant anti-Shiite groups to prevent the spread of Iranian revolutionary thought. Since then, the Shia-Sunni struggle has taken on a life of its own, and hundreds have been killed in assassinations and reprisals. Sectarian militant groups so far have favored violent attack rather than participation in the political process.

In the years following the September 2001 terrorist attacks in New York and Washington, D.C., Pakistan assisted the United States in the war against international terrorism. Between September 2001 and September 2004, Pakistani security forces arrested more than 600 people suspected of being members of al-Qaeda. The military also assisted U.S. operations to capture top al-Qaeda leaders along the Afghanistan border.

However, Pakistan's support of and training for militant groups came under scrutiny. By 2008, American officials had come to believe that leaders of the Pakistani intelligence agency Inter-Services Intelligence (ISI) were tipping off militants so they could avoid capture by U.S. forces in neighboring Afghanistan. There have been several skirmishes between U.S. and Pakistani forces on the Pakistan-Afghanistan border, and many Pakistanis were angered by a May 2011 U.S. special forces raid on Abbottabad, where the terrorist leader Osama bin Laden had been hiding in a compound. The U.S. did not notify Pakistan's government about the operation, in which bin Laden was killed, until after it was over. Pakistanis have also been concerned about the U.S. program of drone attacks on suspected terrorists, which has at times accidentally resulted in civilian casualties.

Afghanistan

Beginning in the 1800s, Afghanistan, a Muslim country that borders Pakistan, thwarted the colonial schemes of both Great Britain and Russia for more than 100 years. In 1979 the Soviet Union invaded the rugged country in support of a communist regime that had seized power there. Over the following decade, Afghanistan was a major battlefield in the Cold War between the Soviet Union and the United States. The United States poured millions of dollars into arms and training for the *mujahedin*, Muslim guerrilla fighters from Afghanistan as well as other parts of the Islamic world. By 1989, unable to suppress mujahedin resistance, Soviet forces withdrew from Afghanistan, leaving a communist regime in place in the capital, Kabul. The leader of that regime agreed to step down in 1992, and an interim government was set up. But stability was not restored.

Rival Afghans fought for power, and former mujahedin commanders established themselves as warlords, controlling their own regions of the countryside. Many of the warlords were involved in illegal activities, and their treatment of the Afghan people was often bad.

A small group of mujahedin, many of them former students

from the Pakistani *madrassas*, began their own resistance campaign. They received aid from Pakistan and came to be known as the Taliban. Many Afghans initially hailed the Taliban as heroes who would rein in the warlords and bring law and order to their war-torn country.

In 1995, however, the Taliban captured Kabul and made it clear that they intended to rule Afghanistan based on their blend of Wahhabist and neo-Deobandi views. By 1996 one of the Taliban's chief supporters, Osama bin Laden, had set up a camp in the Afghan mountains as his home base of operations.

Under the Taliban, official decisions were made in private by leader Mullah Muhammed Omar and a small group of Taliban elders, and the Sharia was implemented by the Ministry for the Promotion of Virtue and Suppression of Vice (PVSV). The PVSV banned television, movies, and non-religious music; rigorously enforced public execution for homosexuality, adultery, and murder; and amputated the limbs of those convicted of robbery. Beating or flogging was prescribed for Afghan men who refused to grow beards and women who refused to wear **burqas**. Women's rights were especially affected under the Taliban. Women were forbidden to work outside the home or receive education, and they could not leave home or seek medical care without a male escort. The Taliban also conducted massacres of the Hazaras, the country's Shiite minority, saying they were not true Muslims.

Muslim religious leaders around the world condemned the Taliban's policies as contrary to Islam. International human rights organizations, Muslim nations from Iran to Egypt, and the U.N. denounced the Taliban for their violations of human rights. By 1999 only three countries—Pakistan, Saudi Arabia, and the United Arab Emirates—had officially recognized the Taliban government.

The Taliban's policies further worsened living conditions in Afghanistan. In 1999 the U.N. Security Council imposed sanctions on the Taliban for refusing to turn over bin Laden, who had been

American troops on patrol in Afghanistan, 2015. US leaders had intended to remove all troops by the end of that year, but concerns about the growth of Taliban influence and related violence led to a decision to maintain combat troops in the country during 2016.

connected with several terrorist attacks against the United States, and Pakistan froze all Taliban assets within its borders. In 2000 the Taliban declared drug use contrary to Islam and banned Afghan farmers from growing poppies (used for the production of opium and heroin), leaving countless farmers and field laborers unemployed. The U.N. imposed further sanctions in 2001 as the Taliban continued to shelter bin Laden. The leadership of the Taliban became divided between those devoted to severe application of the Sharia and those who wanted more moderate laws in order to ease sanctions and address widening poverty in the country.

After the terrorist attacks on September 11, 2001, the United States focused international attention on the Taliban. In October 2001, the United States and Britain began a military campaign against the Taliban, supporting a Afghan faction that opposed the group called the Northern Alliance. By November the Northern Alliance had captured Kabul. The Taliban government collapsed in

December, although both Mullah Omar and Osama bin Laden escaped into a network of caves near the Pakistani border.

With the help of the United Nations, democratic elections were held in Afghanistan in 2004, and Hamid Karzai was chosen to lead the country. However, optimism waned as Karzai's administration failed to adequately combat Afghanistan's problems. Karzai's national government exercised only limited control outside the capital city. The Taliban reemerged as a dangerous force, particularly in the south-central region around Kandahar. Taliban attacks slowed reconstruction efforts and convinced some international aid agencies to pull their workers out of Afghanistan.

With the Taliban and al-Qaeda fighters waging a guerrilla war and launching suicide bombing attacks against American troops as well as government targets in the cities of Afghanistan, a NATO force was instructed to conduct counterinsurgency operations in 2006. Under this program, Afghan and NATO troops would work together to clear insurgents out of a village, then they would rebuild it in hopes that the locals would support the national government, rather than the militants. Just as threatening to national unity was the fact that warlords commanding large, often heavily armed militias (some estimates put the total number of militia members as high as 500,000) were in control of several provinces.

Despite billions of dollars of humanitarian and reconstruction aid from the United States and other donors over the past fifteen years, Afghanistan remains a land of crushing poverty. Sanitation facilities and safe drinking water are largely lacking, health care is scarce, and the education system is in shambles.

Central Asia

Central Asia occupies an area roughly the size of the United States, but has a population of only about 80 million. It became a center of Islamic culture in the 10th century, especially in the Silk Road cities of Bukhara and Samarkand. Sufism later became a major influence. Russian takeover in the 1800s weakened Islamic institutions; Muslims practiced their rituals quietly, mosques were sparse, and the clergy was under the tight control of Russian (and later Soviet) supervisors. Under Soviet president Mikhail Gorbachev's reforms, however, the region saw an Islamic revival.

National identity was a new idea for Central Asians, who had relied on tribal and ethnic affiliations before the Russians took over, and the Soviet-backed governments faced little resistance after the Soviet Union collapsed. However, increasing population, scarcity of land and water, and poverty soon took their toll, opening the way for Islamic militants, many of whom are young and unemployed. Militant fundamentalism thus became one of the most effective ideologies for anti-government opposition. Militant groups have made some inroads in Turkmenistan, Kazakhstan, and Kyrgyzstan, but they have been most successful in Tajikistan and Uzbekistan.

In Tajikistan, the Islamic Revival Party of Tajikistan (IRP) emerged after independence and called for a democracy in which the transition to an Islamic state and the rule of the Sharia would take place gradually. By 1992 conflicts between the Russian-backed government and the IRP, along with ethnic and regional divisions, erupted into a civil war that killed 50,000 and lasted until 1997, at which time Islamic parties were granted a percentage of the seats in the parliament. Aware of the Taliban's misrule and worn down by war and poverty, Tajiks are suspicious of the fundamentalists, but an even more radical party, the Hizb-ut-Tahrir (HUT), is attracting new followers. The Soviet-style government is cracking down, but it seems wary of further empowering the militants by suppressing them too harshly.

Since 1991 Central Asia's largest country, Uzbekistan, has been governed by a Soviet-style leader, Islam Karimov. After claiming the presidency following elections that international observers considered seriously flawed, Karimov used various tactics to extend his term in office. Despite a constitutional prohibition on the president serving more than two terms, Karimov was elected to a third term in 2007 and a fourth term in 2015.

Karimov has conducted crackdowns and issued bans on the fundamentalist militant groups that sprang up after independence. In 1998 the Islamic Movement of Uzbekistan (IMU) declared its goal of establishing an Islamic state in Uzbekistan and eventually all of Central Asia; its leader was based in Peshawar, Pakistan, and had ties to bin Laden. In 1999 the IMU staged numerous incursions into Uzbekistan from its camps in Tajikistan, to which Karimov responded with another crackdown. IMU fighters have assisted the Taliban in Afghanistan in its war against the NATO-backed national government, and have supported Pakistani militants in clashes against government forces. During 2015 IMU leaders publicly pledged allegiance to the Islamic State of Iraq and the Levant (ISIL), and declared that the Islamic Movement of Uzbekistan should be considered part of ISIL.

Karimov's ban against fundamentalist groups means that any Muslim shown to have any connection with the groups can receive a jail sentence, and no Muslim man in the country is allowed to wear a beard, as this is supposedly a sign of fundamentalist leanings.

The political battle against fundamentalist groups has led the United States and its international partners to provide aid to the poor countries of Central Asia. That aid has taken the form of economic support and military assistance in the battle against terrorism.

Southeast Asia

The secular governments of Southeast Asia have prided themselves in recent decades on their pluralism, stability, and great strides toward modernization. But, like other Muslim countries that have experienced rapid growth, they have faced internal problems—poverty, government mismanagement, and religious tensions—that have resulted in fundamentalist opposition.

In recent years, this opposition has led to the growth of terrorist networks in Indonesia, Malaysia, Singapore, and the southern Philippines. Many of these terrorist groups have allegedly been aided by bin Laden. The groups have carried out deadly attacks in Bali, Indonesia, and in the Philippines. In Malaysia they allegedly helped plan the September 11, 2001, attacks on the United States.

A key network is Jemaah Islamiyah, based in Indonesia, which aspires to create an Islamic state that combines the Muslim countries Indonesia, Malaysia, Singapore, and Brunei, together with the Muslim portions of Thailand and the Philippines. Jemaah Islamiyah originally formed in the 1940s to seek the formation of an Islamic state in Indonesia. The group was reinvigorated in the 1990s, when Southeast Asian Muslims returned from fighting with the Afghans against Soviet occupation and brought bin Laden's influence with them. Jemaah Islamiyah has carried out numerous terrorist attacks, including a 2002 bombing at a resort on the Indonesian island of Bali that killed more than 200 people. More recently, in 2014 the group has conducted bombing attacks in the Philippines.

Other networks include the Kumpulan Mujahideen in Malaysia and the Abu Sayyaf and the Moro Islamic Liberation Front (MILF) in the southern Philippines. All condemn the United States for its attacks on Muslims in Iraq, Afghanistan, Syria, and elsewhere. These Asian militants often argue that the United States is in fact the biggest global threat because of its support of Israel and of un-Islamic regimes around the world. The Moro Islamic Liberation Front is based on the island of Mindanao, and had been fighting for independence for the Moro ethnic group. However, in 2011 MILF leaders withdrew their demands for independence, instead saying that they wanted to create an autonomous state for the Moro within the Philippines.

Text-Dependent Questions

1. Who are the Deobandis? What do they believe?

2. Why did the United States begin a military campaign in 2001 to drive the Taliban government from power in Afghanistan?

Research Project

Find out more about the Moro people of the Philippines. How have they been treated in this country? What are their reasons for wanting independence. Write a two-page report and share it with your class.

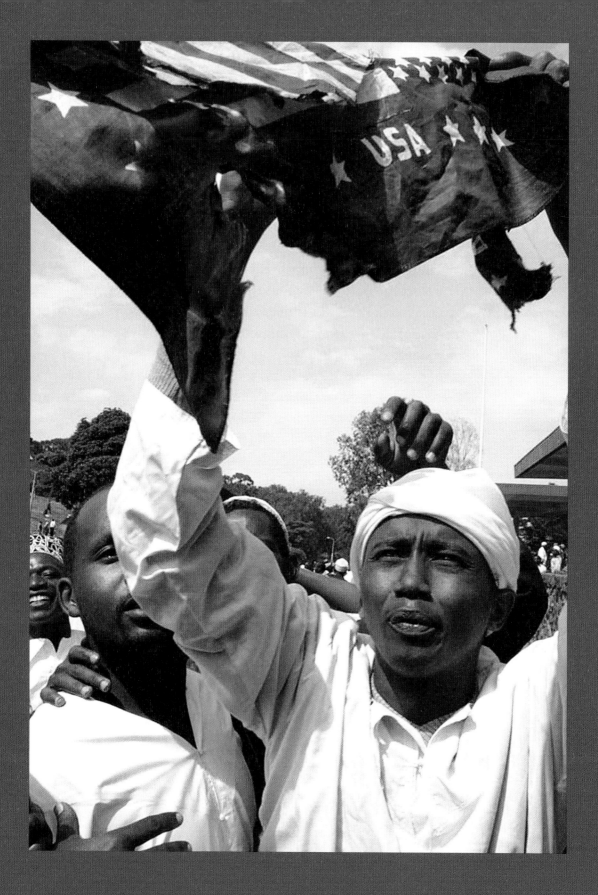

7

Sub-Saharan Africa

Much of northern and east-central Africa, from Morocco in the west to Sudan and Somalia in the east, was absorbed in the early Islamic expansions of the seventh and eighth centuries and has long been considered part of the Arab world. But Muslim communities were established in other parts of Africa as far back as the seventh century. Today, about 15 percent of the world's Muslims, more than 243 million people, live in sub-Saharan Africa, and Islam is the fastest-growing religion on the continent. Nigeria alone has about 75 million Muslims.

Some historians suggest that the most rapid growth of Islam in Africa occurred at the height of European colonialism in the 20th century precisely because Islam provided a different worldview. This same search for an anti-Western alternative has fueled the rise of fundamentalism in the post-colonial and post–Cold War era. As world powers have stopped interfering in the governments of sub-Saharan African nations, corrupt politicians there have suppressed dissent,

Opposite: Members of Kenya's Muslim minority protest their government's adoption of antiterrorism measures that, the protesters say, were masterminded by the United States and discriminate against Muslims.

and poverty and old ethnic divisions have in many cases led to civil war. Social catastrophes, including famine and a growing AIDS crisis, afflict many countries. In countries with large Muslim populations, Islamic fundamentalists have often stepped into the breach, offering demoralized citizens hope for stability amidst the chaos. Nigeria provides the prime example.

Nigeria

In Nigeria, as in the North African countries of Somalia and Sudan, Islamic leaders have implemented the Sharia for a variety of political and spiritual reasons, further complicating the country's already troubled religious, ethnic, and political landscape.

With a population of about 182 million, Nigeria is home to one-sixth of all Africans. Islam arrived in the country with Arab traders in the 13th century, and today approximately 50 percent of Nigerians, mostly of the Hausa and Fulani tribes, are Muslims. Europeans brought Christianity to southern Nigeria in the 15th century, and 40 percent of Nigerians now are Christians; most of them are either Protestants of the Yoruba tribe (in southwest Nigeria) or Roman Catholics of the Ibo tribe (in southeast Nigeria). The remainder of the population holds indigenous beliefs like *animism*.

When Nigeria won its independence from Britain in 1960, its new constitution acknowledged the divisions in the country by creating *autonomous* regions in the east, west, and north. However, this did not end ethnic and religious tensions, and begin-

Words to Understand in This Chapter

animism—the belief that all natural phenomena have souls and can influence human events.

autonomous—a region or section of a country that has a degree of self-government, or freedom from the national government to pursue particular legislative policies.

ning in 1966, civil war resulted in a series of military governments. In addition, huge increases in oil production in the country widened the divide between the wealthy and the poor. Finally, in 1999, Olusegun Obasanjo, a Yoruba Christian from the south, became president in a democratic election and promised to end government corruption and poverty.

In response to Obasanjo's election, the governor of the Nigerian state of Zamfara announced the implementation of Sharia rule, claiming that the switch to Islamic law was needed to stop corruption and poverty. The Sharia has since been implemented in 11 other states, so that approximately one-third of Nigerians now live under its rule. This has increased tensions between the largely Muslim north and the majority Christian south. In fact, since northerners largely dominated Nigerian politics from 1960 until Obasanjo's election, some critics accuse the northern leaders who have implemented the Sharia of deliberately trying to create factions in order to erode the president's influence and increase their own power, both within Nigeria and among oil-rich Arab states. Critics also say that poor people, particularly women, are being scapegoated to illustrate the success of the Sharia, while wealthier citizens and corrupt officials violate the law and go free.

Complicating the situation is the fact that poverty, illiteracy, and poor health care plague most of Nigeria and particularly the predominantly Muslim northern regions. Many Muslims therefore support implementation of the Sharia as a way to improve their living conditions. Their hope is that following Islamic law will increase political and economic stability, but since 1999, more than 6,000 Nigerians have died in religious fighting over Sharia rule. This has deepened the political conflict in the country, and some Muslim leaders have even gone so far as to call for the Sharia states to institute their own army to defend Muslims and the rule of Islamic law.

For centuries, the rulers of walled Muslim cities across northern Nigeria applied the Sharia in both civil and criminal cases.

After the British colonized Nigeria in the late 1800s, however, the Sharia was applied only to personal matters. Now the religious police, known as the *Hizbah*, enforce Islamic law strictly in all areas of life. The penalty for murder is usually death, while the sentence for robbery is often amputation of a limb. Public drinking is punished with flogging, and gambling is also forbidden. Women live under strict conditions in their everyday lives; they must wear the *hijab*, cannot hold a job if they are unmarried, are not allowed to ride on motorcycles (a common mode of travel in Nigeria), have segregated bus stops, and cannot ride on buses with

Amina Lawal (right), convicted by a Nigerian Sharia court of having a child out of wedlock, was sentenced in March 2002 to death by stoning. Amid a swirl of international protests, however, her sentence was overturned the following year.

men. The *Hizbah* have also closed churches and non-Muslim schools, and in 2002 Zamfara began requiring all residents, including non-Muslims, to speak Arabic, a language few citizens know.

Sexual crimes also merit stiff penalties, especially for women. Conviction for sex outside marriage often results in a lashing, while sentencing for adultery can include death. The cases of two women in particular gained international attention. In the state of Sokoto, Safiya Hussaini was found guilty of adultery and sentenced to death by stoning, but after she received global support, the ruling was overturned in early 2002. Also in 2002, in the state of Katsina, Amina Lawal was sentenced to death because she had a child while divorced. (The alleged father of her baby denied having sex with her and the charges against him were dropped.) In September 2003 an appeals court overturned Lawal's death sentence.

In 2009, an Islamic fundamentalist group called Boko Haram ("Western influence is a sin") initiated a terror campaign in northeastern Nigeria that resulted in hundreds of deaths. The campaign ended in July 2009 when government forces stormed Boko Haram's central base and killed the group's leader. But the group soon re-emerged and since 2010 has been waging an insurgency that has resulted in 20,000 deaths and 2.3 million Nigerians displaced from their homes. The group has carried out mass abductions, including the kidnapping of 276 schoolgirls from Chibok in April 2014. In March 2015, leaders of Boko Haram declared their allegiance to the Islamic State of Iraq and the Levant (ISIL).

As the Nigerian government seeks to maintain a democratic process, the implementation of Sharia and the religious and ethnic conflicts continue to complicate the national scene.

The Threat of Terrorism

In addition to Nigeria, many other sub-Saharan governments are plagued by political turmoil, among them Chad, the Republic of

Nigerians protest against Boko Haram, which kidnapped more than 200 girls from a school in Chibok, a Christian village, in May 2014. The non-Muslim girls were forced to convert to Islam. Those who converted were trained to fight or married to Boko Haram fighters; those who refused were sold into slavery.

Congo, Liberia, and Sierra Leone. Many assert that conditions in these countries—erosion of cultural identity, economic deprivation, political repression, and corrupt, mismanaged governments—provide fertile ground for radical fundamentalism to take root and lead to increased terrorist activity.

Even in somewhat more stable states like Kenya, Tanzania, and Mali, government forces are not able to police every area of the country. Observers say that lax security may make sub-Saharan Africa attractive for terrorist groups who want to operate unnoticed and attack vulnerable targets. National borders and inner-city areas are the least secure.

The underdeveloped economies in many African countries may also make it easy to fund terrorism through activities such as money laundering and arms and diamond smuggling. Since terrorist groups operate in secret, however, only fragmentary information is available about their activities in these areas.

Only the future will tell if the chaos in African countries once dominated by Western powers will produce more violent jihadist groups like Boko Haram, or those in the Arab world and Asia.

 Text-Dependent Questions

1. Why did the Nigerian state of Zamfara implement Sharia law in 1999?
2. What is Boko Haram?

 Research Project

Using the Internet or your school library, find out more about the harsh penalties that Sharia law imposes on those who violate its moral precepts, such as amputating limbs or stoning. How have these penalties been imposed in countries like Nigeria? Have national governments allowed Sharia courts to go forward with these punishments? Write a two-page report and share it with your class.

8

The Western Response

For more than two decades, nalysts and ordinary citizens in the West have explored various explanations for why Islamic terrorist organizations are targeting the West. Many of these arguments, however, contradict one another, and no single argument sufficiently explains the complexities of Islamic fundamentalism or the Western response to it.

Some argue for swift and decisive military retaliation without dialogue, while others say the only lasting solution is increased exchange between Westerners and Islamic leaders around the world. Many make broad assumptions about the nature of Islam itself. Some, for example, maintain that Islam and the West are now engaged in a titanic battle between civilizations. Others say Islam is simply incompatible with the modern way of life, while still others argue that Islam is inherently violent and unjust. Some say Islam and democracy can never coexist, while others insist that Islamic democracies will work under the right conditions.

Opposite: These Belgian policemen are on patrol a day after the deadly ISIL March 2016 bombing in Brussels. The rise of the Islamic State, its attacks on Belgium, Paris, Istanbul and other European cities, and its spread of a radical Islamic ideology into Africa and the Middle East, concerns many Westerners.

The central problem with the idea that the West and Islam are locked in an inevitable, global conflict is that Islam, like the West, is not easily defined as a single entity. Islam is in fact made up of Muslims who think differently about the relationship between their faith and politics, just as Westerners have different, shifting ideas about freedom, democracy, and the relationship between church and state. Similarly, the argument that Islam is by nature unjust belies the reality of different legal codes and freedoms in Muslim nations; women, for instance, are thought by some to be oppressed in all Muslim countries, when in fact the status of women varies from one country to the next, and women's status is often as affected by socioeconomic and cultural trends as by Islam. And the arguments that democracy and Islam do or do not mix often overlook the complexities of political rule in Muslim countries, where the chaos of post-colonialism has led to authoritarianism and where democratic projects have not been attempted at all or have been attempted only in ways that deny true participation from opposition groups, including fundamentalists.

However, most observers do agree that the United States and its allies must seriously weigh their responses to Islamic fundamentalism in general and to Islamic terrorist groups in particular. A critical first step in this process is to explore why Muslims, including fundamentalists, around the world think of the West, and particularly the United States, as they do.

 Words to Understand in This Chapter

ethnic cleansing—the mass expulsion or killing of members of an unwanted ethnic or religious group in a society.

hypocrisy—to pretend to be something that you are not; to claim to have certain moral standards or beliefs, but not to follow them in daily behavior.

rhetoric—the art of effective or persuasive speaking or writing.

Muslim Attitudes Toward the West

Doubts among Muslims about Western intentions have their roots in the Crusades of the 11th through 13th centuries and in European expansion beginning in the 19th century and continuing through World War I, when Europeans divided Islamic lands throughout the Middle East and Africa among themselves. This imperialism sowed the seeds for deep mistrust.

Now the preeminent world power is the United States. Though Muslims around the world admire American principles, many accuse the United States of *hypocrisy*. These Muslims say that, while the United States is not overtly colonizing Muslim lands, in its dealings with the Muslim world it fails to apply the principles it holds dear for its own citizens.

In the Muslim view, the high point of U.S. hypocrisy is its uncritical support for Israel. This issue, more than any other, unites Muslims around the world in their mistrust of the United States. Surveys in the Arab world show that a majority of Muslims feel that the Palestinian issue is an important, or even the most important, issue they face as Muslims; surveys of Muslims in the United States show strong support for a Palestinian state. As the United States supports what Muslims view as Israel's repressive policies in the occupied territories and looks the other way while Israel violates U.N. resolutions, Muslims cry foul and accuse the United States of ignoring its own principles when convenient.

Similar charges of hypocrisy have been leveled at the United States for imposing sanctions against Iran for its nuclear weapons program, without requiring that nations like India and Israel terminate their own programs. Muslims also condemn what they view as the slow response of the United States to Serbian campaigns of *ethnic cleansing* against Bosnian Muslims and Kosovar Muslims during the 1990s, as well as the U.S. refusal to take strong action to halt the repression of Muslims in places like Kashmir and Chechnya.

Protesters in India demonstrate against what they perceive as US and Israeli imperialism just before American President Barack Obama was scheduled to visit the country in January 2015.

While many Islamic fundamentalists decry Western influence in general, the vast majority of Muslims around the world do not see Westerners as evil. However, some suggest that the *rhetoric* of good versus evil as a way to increase support for the West's "war on terror" may have the effect, intentional or not, of increasing mistrust among Muslims worldwide.

The History of the U.S. Response

U.S. policy toward Islamic fundamentalism first took shape during World War II, when President Franklin D. Roosevelt sent U.S. troops to protect Saudi Arabia. This close relationship continued through the Cold War and the 1970s and 1980s, even as the two countries disagreed over Israel. In 1990 the United States based a military force in Saudi Arabia that numbered in the thousands and remained until 2003, when all but a few hundred troops were pulled out. The ties with the Saudi government have given the United States access to the vast oil reserves in the Persian Gulf region and a base for operations against Iraq during the 1991 and 2003 conflicts. The United States has continued this relationship in spite of international condemnation of the Saudi monarchy's violations of human rights. The Saudi government has also been a primary sponsor, using its enormous oil funds, of fundamentalist Islamic movements worldwide, including militant groups like Hamas and the Taliban, and to a Sunni insurgency in Yemen.

In spite of its intimate relationship with Saudi Arabia, after the Iranian revolution of 1979 the United States gradually began to shift from its Cold War opposition to Arab nationalists to a fight against Islamic fundamentalism as a political force. After Khomeini came to power, fundamentalist groups throughout the Islamic world stepped up their criticism of Western influence, while militant groups actively resisted pro-West governments and the United States itself. The West was shocked when militants in Tehran held 49 American embassy workers hostage for 444 days, and the Iranian-backed attacks against U.S. and French troops in Beirut in 1983, which killed more than 300 soldiers, brought the suicide bombing into American consciousness.

Many U.S. policy makers began to concentrate on Islamic extremism as representative of Islam in general, and the United States supported a number of the nationalist governments it had once opposed as they suppressed more moderate fundamentalist groups that sought to participate in the political process. From Egypt to Indonesia, from Algeria to the Philippines, national leaders repressed fundamentalist resistance, and in the process won U.S. military and economic aid. In many instances, however, the repressive response of these governments only strengthened and further radicalized fundamentalist groups.

Meanwhile, the Cold War between the United States and the

Soviet Union also fueled the growth of militant Islamic fundamentalism. While the administration of President Ronald Reagan had attempted to isolate Iran for its fundamentalist leadership, it actively funded the training of the 20,000-strong mujahedin in Afghanistan to contain Soviet expansion in the region. The nucleus of current international Islamic terrorist networks was in many ways formed in that conflict, when fighters were trained in Pakistan and thousands of Arabs fought in Afghanistan under the influence of Osama bin Laden, who himself had strong connections with the U.S. Central Intelligence Agency at that time. After the Soviet withdrawal, the United States disengaged from Afghanistan as well, and many Arab fighters felt betrayed. They subsequently returned to their own countries to establish or contribute to militant movements there. The United States then put pressure on the governments of Muslim countries to rein in these militant movements, to which some leaders responded with frustration given that the United States had itself earlier financed the militants.

In 1991 the United States and a coalition that included European and Persian Gulf states expelled Iraq from Kuwait, which Iraq had invaded the previous year. While oil-rich Persian Gulf governments did aid the war effort, many Muslims within these countries and throughout the world protested the U.S.-led attack on a Muslim country. Combined with rising tensions in Israel and the occupied territories, where Palestinians had begun the first *intifada*, the Gulf War and the presence of American and European soldiers on Saudi Arabian soil reinforced Islamic fundamentalists' belief in the anti-Muslim, interventionist intentions of the West.

President Bill Clinton continued President George Bush's pursuit of secure access to oil, though he did promote the 1993 Oslo Accords between Israel and the PLO, and he more carefully distinguished between moderate and militant fundamentalists. Concerns about Islamic extremism rose rapidly, however, as terrorist attacks increased through the 1990s. Among the targets bombed were the World Trade Center in 1993, U.S. military installations in Saudi

Turkish demonstrators protest against the publication of cartoons in a Dutch magazine that mocked the Prophet Muhammad, 2006.

Arabia in 1996, the American embassies in Kenya and Tanzania in 1998, and the USS *Cole* in Yemen in 2000. Osama bin Laden was suspected to be behind these attacks, and after his name appeared on the FBI's Most Wanted list in 1998, the United States bombed his training camps in Afghanistan and Somalia. More and more, Western lawmakers and policy analysts interpreted the Muslim world through the lens of extremist activity.

American Response

In the wake of the terrorist attacks on September 11, 2001, Western policies on Islamic fundamentalism have increasingly been characterized by two strains of thought. The first blames Islamic fundamentalists, rather than secular regimes, for the widespread lack of development and democracy in the Muslim world and for the terrorist networks now threatening Western targets. This strain of thought favors crackdowns on fundamentalist movements. The second strain of thought advocates diplomacy to encourage more open political processes in Muslim countries and thereby decrease terrorist activity.

The administration of President George W. Bush was largely characterized by the more confrontational approach. After September 11, 2001, President Bush immediately declared an international "war on terror" to wipe out the threat of terrorism worldwide, and the U.N. Security Council passed a resolution condemning the attacks on U.S. soil and calling on all nations to bring those behind the attacks to justice. In an effort to root out Osama bin Laden, a U.S.-led coalition invaded Afghanistan just two months after the September attacks. When the United States and Britain invaded Iraq in March 2003, the justification for the war rested largely on the assertion that Saddam Hussein had weapons of mass destruction that he might shift to terrorist groups. Numerous European countries, including France and Germany, condemned the invasion of Iraq, while Muslim fundamentalists around the world interpreted the latest use of Western military force as a fresh assault on Islam, a view that some observers predict could have the effect of increasing rather than weakening the appeal of fundamentalist movements.

The Obama administration reversed some of the Bush policies, taking a more conciliatory approach toward the Muslim world. In 2009 President Obama delivered a speech in Cairo about the relationship of Islam and the West that was well-received. Obama also began to withdraw American troops from Iraq and Afghanistan, although the president soon found that he could not completely pull out of these countries as radicals raced to fill the void left by the troops and destabilized the countries.

Meanwhile, international human rights groups became concerned that the war on terror gave leaders in numerous countries an excuse to severely repress Islamic fundamentalist groups. In Central Asia, the leaders of Tajikistan, Uzbekistan, and Kazakhstan are taking a harder line against opposition groups as the United States funds a stronger military presence in the region. Concerns were also raised about clampdowns on alleged terrorist activities in Chechnya, Egypt, Malaysia, and Saudi Arabia and anti-terror laws passed in Indonesia, India, Singapore, and Tanzania. Even the American prison facility for jihadists at Guantanamo Bay, Cuba, which President Obama vowed to close, has remained open throughout nearly all of his eight years in office.

As the threat of terrorism continues, the challenge for the United States and other Western countries will be to deal with the complexities within fundamentalist Islam and within Islam itself. Future policy makers will continue to choose between the use of military and financial strength to stop fundamentalist movements and the exercise of diplomacy to encourage more open political processes and economic development in Muslim countries.

 # Text-Dependent Questions

1. Why do some Muslims accuse the United States of hypocrisy?
2. What event in 1979 helped to shift American attitudes toward political Islam?

 # Research Project

Video is available online of President Barack Obama's June 2009 speech to the Muslim world, titled "A New Beginning." Watch the video, then write down your thoughts. What is the point of the president's Cairo speech? How does he attempt to reach out to Muslims? Do you think Obama accomplished what he hoped to with the speech? Write two paragraphs summarizing your feelings about the speech, and share them with your class.

Chronology

1303	Taqi al-Din Ahmad ibn Taymiyya instructs Muslims to revolt against their Mongol rulers for not being faithful to Islam.
1745	Muhammad ibn Abd al-Wahhab and Muhammad ibn Saud forge an alliance.
1924	The Ottoman Empire collapses and the caliphate is abolished.
1928	Hasan al-Banna establishes the Muslim Brotherhood in Egypt.
1932	Saudi Arabia is established as the first modern Islamic state.
1938	Oil is discovered in Saudi Arabia.
1941	Mawlana Mawdudi establishes the Islamic Society of India.
1947	Pakistan is founded as a country for Muslims.
1948	Israel becomes a nation.
1965	Sayyid Qutb publishes his book *Milestones* in Egypt; he is executed one year later.
1967	Israel defeats Egypt, Jordan, and Syria in the Six-Day War.
1973	Egypt wins some battles in the 1973 October War with Israel, and OPEC stages an oil embargo.
1979	Ayatollah Ruhollah Khomeini declares Iran an Islamic state; Soviet troops occupy Afghanistan.
1987	The first Palestinian *intifada* against the Israeli presence in the West Bank and Gaza Strip begins; Hamas is founded.
1991	The United States defeats Iraq in the Gulf War and keeps U.S. troops in Saudi Arabia.
1996	The Taliban takes control of Afghanistan.
2000	The second Palestinian *intifada* begins, damaging the Israeli-Palestinian peace process.
2001	Terrorist attacks on U.S. soil kill more than 3,000, and the United States invades Afghanistan and overthrows the Taliban.

Chronology

2003   The United States invades Iraq and topples the secular government of Saddam Hussein.

2008   In November, members of the Islamist terrorist group Lashkar-e-Taiba attack multiple sites in Mumbai, India. More than 250 people are killed.

2012   Mohamed Morsi, a member of the Muslim Brotherhood, is sworn in as president after he wins Egypt's first competitive presidential election. Morsi would be ousted in June of the following year by a military coup.

2013   Islamist groups fighting in Iraq and Syria form the Islamic State of Iraq and the Levant (ISIL), which is able to capture and hold territory in both countries.

2014   In June, the Islamic State of Iraq and the Levant declares a caliphate in the territory they control. They rename their group Islamic State (IS), although most Western observers continue to refer to the group as ISIL.

2015   The United States and other Western nations strike an agreement with the Islamic Republic of Iran, in which they agree to lift economic sanctions and restrictions on oil sales in exchange for Iran eliminating its program to build nuclear weapons. Throughout the year, terrorists who claim allegiance to ISIL commit numerous attacks, including the destruction of a airliner from Egypt carrying more than 200 Russian citizens, and mass shootings in Paris that kill 130 people.

2016   Tensions between Iran and Saudi Arabia rise after King Salman orders the execution of a Shiite cleric, Nimr al-Nimr, along with 46 other dissidents.

🔑 Series Glossary

BCE **and** CE—alternatives to the traditional Western designation of calendar eras, which used the birth of Jesus as a dividing line. BCE stands for "Before the Common Era," and is equivalent to BC ("Before Christ"). Dates labeled CE, or "Common Era," are equivalent to Anno Domini (AD, or "the Year of Our Lord").

hadith—the body of customs, sayings, and traditions ascribed to the prophet Muhammad and his closest companions in the early Muslim community, as recorded by those who witnessed them.

hajj—the fifth pillar of Islam; a pilgrimage to Mecca, which all Muslims who are able are supposed to make at least once in their lifetime.

imam—a Muslim spiritual leader. In the Sunni tradition, an imam is a religious leader who leads the community in prayer. In the Shiite tradition, an imam is a descendant of Muhammad who is the divinely chosen and infallible leader of the community.

jihad—struggle. To Muslims, the "greater jihad" refers to an individual's struggle to live a pure life, while the "lesser jihad" refers to defensive struggle or warfare against oppression and the enemies of Islam.

Qur'an—Islam's holy scriptures, which contain Allah's revelations to the prophet Muhammad in the early seventh century.

Sharia—a traditional system of Islamic law based on the Qur'an, the opinion of Islamic leaders, and the desires of the community.

Shia—one of the two major sects of Islam; members of this sect are called Shiites.

Sufism—a mystical tradition that emphasizes the inner aspect of spirituality through meditation and remembrance of God.

Sunna—the traditions of the prophet Muhammad as exemplified by his actions and words, and preserved in the Qur'an and Hadith.

Sunni—the largest sect of Islam; the name is derived from the Arabic phrase "the Path," referring to those who follow the instructions of Muhammad as recorded in the Qur'an and other ancient writings or traditions.

umma—the worldwide community of Muslims.

Further Reading

Ayoob, Mohammed. *The Many Faces of Political Islam: Religion and Politics in the Muslim World*. Ann Arbor: University of Michigan Press, 2008.

Bergen, Peter L. *United States of Jihad: Examining America's Homegrown Terrorists*. New York: Crown, 2016.

Byman, Daniel. *Al Qaeda, the Islamic State, and the Global Jihadist Movement*. New York: Oxford University Press, 2015.

Gabriel, Mark A. *Islam and Terrorism*. Lake Mary: Fla.: Front Line, 2015.

Harris, Sam, and Maajid Nawaz. *Islam and the Future of Tolerance: A Dialogue*. Cambridge, Mass.: Harvard University Press, 2015.

McCants, William. *The ISIS Apocalypse: The History, Strategy, and Doomsday Vision of the Islamic State*. New York: St. Martin's Press, 2015.

Mandaville, Peter. *Islam and Politics*. New York: Routledge, 2014.

Mansfield, Peter. *A History of the Middle East*. 4th ed. revised and updated by Nicholas Pelham. New York: Penguin Books, 2013.

Martin, Richard C., and Abbas Barzegar, eds. *Islamism: Contested Perspectives on Political Islam*. Stanford, Calif.: Stanford University Press, 2010.

Osman, Tarek. *Islamism: What it Means for the Middle East and the World*. New Haven, Conn.: Yale University Press, 2016.

Internet Resources

http://islam.com

A portal with information about Islam, including discussion forums, articles, and links to other resources.

http://america.aljazeera.com

The English-language website of the Arabic news service Al Jazeera provides articles and videos on breaking news, as well as feature stories that provide background material, including profiles of leaders and essays reacting to major events.

https://sacredsites.com/middle_east/iran/shia_islam.html

An essay on the history of holy places in Islam, and how Muslims of different sects treat such shrines.

http://www.fordham.edu/halsall/islam/islamsbook.html

Fordham University provides this online Islamic History Sourcebook, with links to texts from every period in the history of Islam, as well as maps and other resources.

http://www.cair.com/

The Council on American-Islamic Relations (CAIR) is an organization dedicated to providing an Islamic perspective on issues of importance to the American people.

http://www.newsweek.com/short-history-islamism-298235

This *Newsweek* magazine essay provides a short history of Islamism.

Index

Numbers in **bold italic** refer to captions.

Index

Index

Index

Index

Picture Credits

Contributors

Senior Consultant CAMILLE PECASTAING, PH.D., is acting director of the Middle East Studies Program at the Paul H. Nitze School of Advanced International Studies at Johns Hopkins University. A student of behavioral sciences and historical sociology, Dr. Pecastaing's research focuses on the cognitive and emotive foundations of xenophobic political cultures and ethnoreligious violence, using the Muslim world and its European and Asian peripheries as a case study. He has written on political Islam, Islamist terrorism, social change, and globalization. Pecastaing's essays have appeared in many journals, including World Affairs and Policy Review. He is the author of *Jihad in the Arabian Sea* (Hoover Institution Press, 2011).

General Editor DR. JOHN CALVERT is assistant professor of history at Creighton University. He is interested in social protest and political resistance movements in the Arab world during the 19th and 20th centuries, and his current research focuses on the intellectual career and cultural milieu of Sayyid Qutb (1906–1966), the prominent Egyptian ideologue of Islamism.

A member of the faculty at Creighton since 1994, Dr. Calvert teaches a variety of courses relating to the medieval and modern periods of Middle East history. He earned a Ph.D. in Islamic Studies from McGill University in Montreal. His published articles include "Mythic Foundations of Radical Islam" (*Orbis*, Winter 2004); "Sayyid Qutb and the Power of Political Myth: Insights from Sorel" (*Historical Reflections/Reflexions Historiques*, 2004); "The Islamist Syndrome of Cultural Confrontation" (*Orbis*, Spring 2002); and "The Nation and the Individual: Sayyid Qutb's Tifl min al-Qarya (Child from the Village)" (*The Muslim World*, Spring 2000).

LILAH EL-SAYED is a writer, editor, and teacher. She lives in Minnesota with her husband and son.